IMAGES
of America

THE SHAKERS OF
UNION VILLAGE

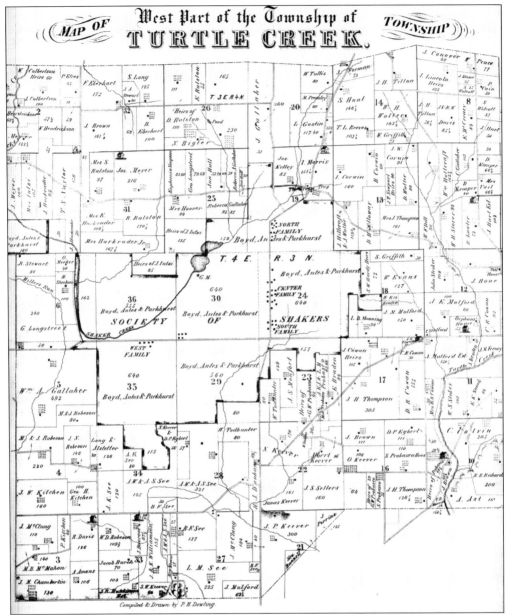

In the 1875 Warren County atlas, Union Village was shown as the Society of Shakers. Trustee Peter Boyd, Elder Philip Antes, and Elder Amos Parkhurst are listed as owners of the property. The dots surrounding the West, Center, South, and North families represent the dwellings, laundries, shops, farm buildings, and tenant houses attached to each group. At the time, 215 Shakers lived and worked in the 4,509-acre community. Their land was valued at $286,000 and their personal property at $31,000. (Warren County Historical Society.)

On the cover: Please see page 54. (Otterbein-Lebanon Archives.)

IMAGES
of America

THE SHAKERS OF UNION VILLAGE

Cheryl Bauer

ARCADIA
PUBLISHING

Published by Arcadia Publishing
Charleston SC, Chicago IL, Portsmouth NH, San Francisco CA

Printed in the United States of America

Library of Congress Catalog Card Number: 2007922282

For all general information contact Arcadia Publishing at:
Telephone 843-853-2070
Fax 843-853-0044
E-mail sales@arcadiapublishing.com
For customer service and orders:
Toll-Free 1-888-313-2665

Visit us on the Internet at www.arcadiapublishing.com

Mary Lue Warner, archivist at Otterbein Lebanon Retirement Community, works at the desk of Dr. Joseph M. Phillippi, a founder of the Otterbein Home, in this 2006 photograph. Warner has been instrumental in creating a Shaker Room and Attic Museum in the Shakers' original office building as well as researching, speaking, and writing about Union Village. This book is dedicated to her. (Author's collection.)

CONTENTS

ACKNOWLEDGMENTS

In 1999, Rob Portman introduced me to the Shakers of Union Village. At the time, Portman was a congressman from Ohio with an abiding interest in Shaker history. His grandparents Robert H. and Virginia Jones began to gather Union Village lore and artifacts in 1926, just 14 years after the village's demise. Since then, the Jones-Portman family has been instrumental in sharing Union Village's story and its importance to American history.

Portman and I wrote the first comprehensive history of the community, *Wisdom's Paradise: The Forgotten Shakers of Union Village*, in time for the village's bicentennial in 2005. Since then, many rare and previously unpublished images and documents pertaining to the Shakers have surfaced. These materials tell Union Village's story in a compelling and graphic way.

I am truly indebted to Mary Lue Warner, archivist of the Otterbein Lebanon Retirement Community (which exists at the original Union Village site), and Mary Klei, curator of the Warren County Historical Society Museum in Lebanon, for their help in creating this book.

Other generous contributors are Dr. C. Nelson Melampy; Dr. M. Stephen and Miriam R. Miller; Larrie Curry, Shakertown at Pleasant Hill, Harrodsburg, Kentucky; Tommy Hines, South Union Shaker Museum, South Union, Kentucky; and Sabine Kretzschmar, the Shaker Museum, Shaker Heights, Ohio.

Thanks also to Patricia Grove and James Zimmerlin of the Edna L. Bowyer Records Center and Archives of Warren County, Shirley Ray and Deanna Campbell of the Warren County Historical Society, and Leon Bey and Joyce Grabill of the Friends of Watervliet, Ohio, Shaker Village. Others who provided materials, information, and guidance include Michael Anderson, Zane Bauer, Dennis Dalton, Sue Frery of the Warren County Genealogical Society, Carol Gabriel and Tom Stander of the Butler County Historical Society, Joan Baxter of the Greene County Historical Society, Nancy R. Horlacher and Elli Bambakidis of the Dayton Metro Library, Andy Sewall and Pat Bennett of Hard Lines Designs, Christian Goodwillie of Hancock Shaker Village, and Janet Stuckey of Miami University Libraries.

My deepest appreciation goes to my husband, Randy McNutt, for his inexhaustible enthusiasm and scanning skills.

INTRODUCTION

When Shaker missionaries from Mount Lebanon, New York, arrived at Turtle Creek in Warren County in March 1805, they found a group of spiritually inquisitive Christians living in a lush river valley. The missionaries planted the seeds of Shakerism in the hearts of two of the settlement's most influential members, Malcolm Worley and Pastor Richard McNemar. The beginnings of a fruitful religious community—unlike any other west of the Allegheny Mountains—were planted soon after.

The settlement became Union Village, the first Shaker community in the West. Worley and McNemar helped create a Shaker renaissance that, within the following 20 years, saw the start of six other Shaker villages in Ohio, Kentucky, and Indiana, and sparked a flurry of compositions and publications that helped define Shakerism for much of the 19th century. Union Village also became a leader in horticultural and agricultural industries. By the time the settlement disbanded in 1912 due to economics, declining membership, and societal change, it had been one of the most productive and populous Shaker communities in history.

Shakers traced their origins to Mother Ann Lee, a working-class Quaker in 18th-century England who broke from Quaker fellowship to pursue a more personal form of Christianity. Lee and eight followers fled religious persecution in England to come to America in 1774. They settled near Albany, New York, in what became the Watervliet community.

Lee's followers eventually shaped her religious precepts into a sect called the United Society of Believers in Christ's Second Appearing. Members referred to themselves as Believers. The world derisively called them Shakers because of their intense shaking and dancing during worship. It was a name the Believers accepted over the years and the name that has since been borrowed to describe an esthetic style.

Their lives centered on the belief that God had both a female and male side, meaning that men and women were equal in worth and ability. Believers revered Jesus as the best example of Christian life for men to follow and Lee as the best role model for women. They believed that Jesus had been the first instance of the Christ, or teacher spirit, coming to mankind, and that Lee was the second appearance of the Christ spirit.

Lee's ministry marked the Millennium, a period when Believers should live as the angels do while waiting for the physical return of Christ. For that reason, Believers were to be celibate, as brothers and sisters. Marital and biological ties were transformed as Believers' new spiritual lives began. This doctrine led to the greatest opposition to Shakerism in the 19th century as non-Shaker family members often tried to persuade relatives to leave the sect, and in some cases, removed members by force.

Early Shakers also faced criticism—and sometimes persecution—because they practiced racial equality, pacifism, and a communal lifestyle. Believers who signed the United Society covenant gave all their worldly possessions to the sect's joint interest, or common economy. Would-be heirs often challenged the covenant in court, but it typically was upheld.

Union Village, like other Shaker communities, was divided into several lots or families. Each family consisted of men and women who maintained separate rooms in large dwellings on their lot. Each family had its own businesses, shops, barns, fields, and gardens. Children lived in their own dwelling, cared for by several sisters. They attended the village school and learned various skills and occupations from the adults. In the antebellum West, Union Village presented a safe, productive refuge for many orphans and homeless people. Children could choose to stay or leave when they became young adults. For anyone willing to abide by the Shakers' rules, it was a good life. A free education; a warm, clean home; ample food; an occupation; and a spiritual family appealed to many people.

By the middle of the 19th century, Union Village had become renown for its champion livestock, garden seed industry, and herbal medicines. As the Shakers became more involved in the local economy, their religious views were better tolerated. Union Village had also benefited from the start from support by a progressive, influential group of citizens who saw the Shakers as exercising the religious freedom that had been won in the Revolutionary War.

By the early 20th century, a changing society and declining membership led to the closing of several Shaker villages in the West and in New England. The United Brethren Church purchased Union Village in 1912 as a home for needy children and the aged. Other villages continued to close during the 20th century. Some communities were absorbed into their regions, such as North Union, near Cleveland, which became the community of Shaker Heights. Others such as Pleasant Hill, Kentucky, and Hancock, Massachusetts, became impressive living museums. As of 2007, one Shaker community remains active: Sabbathday Lake, near Gloucester, Maine. Two sisters and two brothers live there, quietly practicing their faith and sharing their culture with visitors.

When the United Brethren Church purchased Union Village, fewer than 20 Believers still lived there. Those members moved into the village's office building, which had been extensively remodeled in the 1890s in an unsuccessful attempt to attract new members. The United Society of Believers' central ministry appointed several sisters from the Canterbury, New Hampshire, Shaker community to come to Union Village to care for those people.

Meanwhile, the United Brethren leaders began cleaning up the grounds and refurbishing and remodeling Shaker structures into facilities to provide homes for children and the elderly. In many ways, the new Otterbein Home of 1913 resembled the old Shaker village. Children were living in group homes, cared for by trusted adults. They attended school in the community and participated in worship. Elderly people were assured of a safe, comfortable home. The Otterbein Home became a community of all ages, with each person being valued.

Farming and livestock production, which the aging Shakers had turned over to tenant farmers, were revitalized with increased stock and more fields being cultivated. Tenant farmers, trained by the Shakers, still worked the farm.

Unfortunately many of the Shaker structures were demolished over the years as they became uninhabitable. With an increasing population to care for, Otterbein leaders chose to build more suitable residential units and administrative offices.

Today however, two of the most prominent Shaker buildings remain in use on the Otterbein campus. They are open for tours by appointment. For arrangements, call 513-932-2020.

The office, nicknamed Marble Hall due to the addition of many marble features during the 1890s renovation, is home to the Otterbein Shaker Room and Attic Museum area. Shaker features are visible throughout the building, including the basement where workmanship from 1810 is evident.

New Bethany Hall, completed in 1846, may also be visited. The Shakers fired over a million bricks on site to construct the building, which was the largest dwelling in the village and said to be the largest brick structure in Ohio at the time.

More Shaker artifacts and history are available at the Warren County Historical Society Museum and at the Golden Lamb Inn in Lebanon.

One

THE EARLY YEARS

Vincy McNemar was a child when Shaker missionaries arrived at the Turtle Creek community near Beedle's Station in Warren County in March 1805. Her father, Richard McNemar, was pastor of the Turtle Creek Church, which had recently separated from the Presbyterian Church to join the New Light movement. After Richard accepted the Shaker faith that April, his congregation followed him. Vincy and most of her six siblings also became Shakers. She became a noted writer of sacred songs. (Warren County Historical Society.)

Whereas, we the Subscribers, near Lebanon, in the County of Warren and State of Ohio, being members of the Community of people, in the world, known and distinguished by the name of Shakers, having received the grace of God, in this day of Christ's second appearance, which has separated us from the course and connections of this world, to take up our cross and follow Christ in the regeneration; believing it to be our duty and privilege to spend the rest of our days and talents for the support and increase of the Gospel, which we believe to be the only way of salvation. And we believe it to be our duty, as far as in us lies, to live peaceably with all men; and especially with one another, endeavoring to build up each other in the Truth; and not to do any thing, that tends to discord or disunion. And Whereas a number of us, who profess to be of one Faith, are desirous to live together in one family for the upbuilding, protection and safety of each other; and for the right understanding (according to law and custom) of all and singular, whom this may concern; do, therefore, according to our own faith and voluntary covenant and agree to live

Five adults signed this covenant to live together in the Shaker faith for "the upbuilding, protection and safety of each other" on December 22, 1806. The agreement marked the beginning of communal life at Turtle Creek for the new Shaker converts. Shakers had begun living in small communal families in England in the 1760s out of financial necessity. The lifestyle supported the Shaker goal of celibate lives as brothers and sisters in Christ. It gradually became the norm for Shakers. Malcolm Worley, the first Shaker convert west of the Alleghenies, led the Turtle Creek Family. Their aim was to "use and improve our strength, abilities and faculties for the benefit and support of each other." They affirmed they had all joined the sect voluntarily and that any of them were free to leave if they wished. Some people were suspicious of the Shakers' unconventional lifestyle. Over the years, however, most people grew to admire them for their ethics, charity, and sincerity. (Edna L. Bowyer Records Center and Archives of Warren County.)

together in the family, now under the care and
and direction of Malcom Worley, and all and
each of us to use and improve our strength, abilities and faculties for the benefit and support
of each other; without ever having any demand
upon, or bringing any debt or blame against any
member of said family, or against any of those of
us, that so covenant together; on account of any
favor or benefit bestowed (in sickness or in health,
or an account of any labor or service; that has
been, or may be done by us.
          And Whereas we believe it is our pri-
velege to be a free people; therefore we do Agree
that whenever any of us shall think it best not to live
together any longer, then we shall signify the
same to said Malcom, and if it still continue
to be our faith to seperate, then we shall be
at full liberty so to do, ever exercising the free
dom of our own consciences, and voluntary choice;
but always to leave each other free from all
debt or demands, which is our present faith
and Covenant.
                    In Testimony of which, we
have hereunto set our hands and seals this
22d day of December 1806.
In the presence of

Although the Worley agreement was signed in 1806, it was not filed in the Warren County Common Pleas Court until February 8, 1811. Robert Wilson, one of the original signers, wanted out of the sect, and either he or his heirs wanted to regain property he had signed over to the Shakers. It was a scenario played out numerous times over Union Village's first four decades. The United Society of Believers, which encompassed all Shakers, had covenants with each individual Shaker village and its respective members who signed the agreement. People could live in a Shaker community without signing the covenant, but those who signed were considered full members who legally gave all their possessions and property to the United Society. The courts upheld Shaker covenants in the majority of 19th-century cases. (Edna L. Bowyer Records Center and Archives of Warren County.)

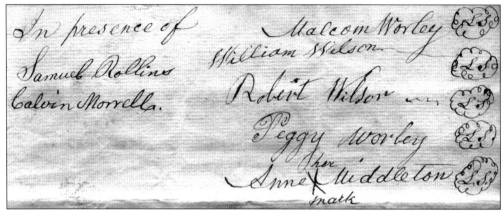

The Worley agreement was signed by Malcolm and his wife, Peggy, Turtle Creek landowners William Wilson and Robert Wilson, and Anna Middleton. Middleton was the second western Shaker convert and a 19-year-old former slave from Virginia. Samuel Rollins and Calvin Morrell, early Union Village leaders, witnessed the signings. Middleton could only make her mark at the time, but by the 1820s, night classes for women were held at Union Village to help all members become literate. (Edna L. Bowyer Records Center and Archives of Warren County.)

Malcolm and Peggy Worley's frame home was the largest dwelling at Turtle Creek and the initial stop for Shaker missionaries in 1805. When the Worley agreement was signed in 1806, 15 people were living there, resulting in the construction of a nearby communal dwelling. (Warren County Historical Society.)

David Darrow and Francis Dunlavy's signatures on this 1810 court document foreshadow the influence that these two men had during Union Village's first 20 years. Darrow was a prominent elder sent from the New Lebanon, New York, central ministry in 1805 to lead the western converts. Under Darrow's leadership, the western Shaker communities soon grew to match the eastern villages in size, population, and productivity. Francis Dunlavy, a prominent Lebanon citizen was the brother of Shaker elder John Dunlavy. Francis provided legal advice to the Shakers and defended their religious rights. Francis's influence in Warren County helped somewhat to counteract early negative public opinion about the Shakers. In 1810, Francis was a common pleas court judge set to hear the case of Robert Wilson, who had left the Shakers, against Darrow. In the document, Darrow asks that the case be delayed until Elder Malcolm Worley returns from a missionary trip to Kentucky to testify for the Shakers. (Edna L. Bowyer Records Center and Archives of Warren County.)

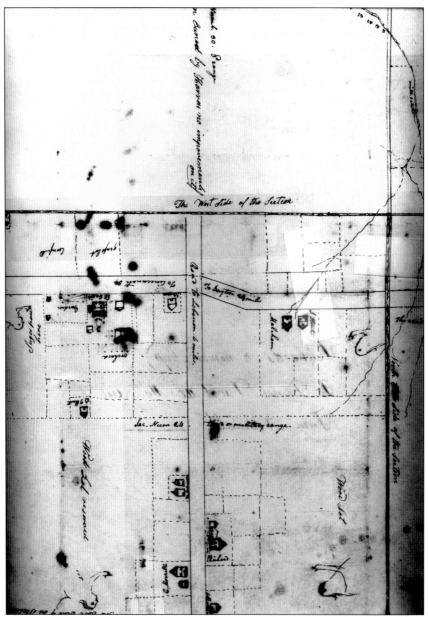

Richard McNemar drew this map of the Turtle Creek community around 1806. The other homeowners shown, who had also become Shakers, were Samuel Rollins, David Johnson, Thomas Hunt, John Cassen, and Malcolm Worley, who became the first Shaker convert west of the Allegheny Mountains on March 27, 1805. At this time, the new converts still lived with their spouses and children in their family homes. As the community grew over the following five years, communal dwellings, patterned after those of Shakers in New England and New York State, began to be built. Shakers believed they were living in the Millennial Age and therefore should live purely as the angels do in heaven. Spouses were instructed to be celibate as brothers and sisters. Men and women occupied the same dwellings in their respective spiritual families, but lived in separate quarters. Children were cared for communally in the Children's Order. (Otterbein-Lebanon Archives.)

Three figures dance on a platform between Richard McNemar's main cabin and kitchen cabin in his 1806 drawing. Dancing was an integral part of Shaker worship but an oddity to Warren County's other religious groups. Arsonists destroyed the dancing platform in September 1805 but converts quickly rebuilt it. A variety of sacred dances became part of the Shaker tradition, with all ages being encouraged to participate. (Otterbein-Lebanon Archives.)

The *Kentucky Revival*, published in Cincinnati in 1807, was Richard McNemar's account of an 1800 religious revival, which he believed set the stage for Shakerism in the West. McNemar's acceptance of Shakerism encouraged hundreds of more conversions from 1805 until his death in 1839. He wrote scores of poems, pamphlets, and hymns, and also represented the Shakers in legal matters. (Warren County Historical Society.)

The tool chest that Richard McNemar made for his son Benjamin around 1808 is noteworthy for several reasons. As the new Shakers grew in their religion, they were to eschew personal possessions and treat all children as their own. Yet as a father, McNemar wanted to make something special for his son. McNemar is thought to have added the label on the back of the piece. (Warren County Historical Society.)

McNemar's walnut and pine chest for his son is also special in its graceful design and attention to details. McNemar embraced the Shaker precept of doing all tasks as well as possible to glorify God. In addition to being a leader and writer, he made hundreds of chairs, spinning wheels, and related items as a Shaker. (Warren County Historical Society.)

By 1813, when this document was written, the Turtle Creek community numbered 319 people who now called the settlement Union Village. In the three-page document, the Shakers whose names appeared notified Warren County authorities that they were naming Shaker trustee John Wallace as their agent to collect and distribute any profit they made from their labors. Members who fully committed themselves and their property to the United Society of Believers signed a church covenant that proved legally binding in several court cases over the 19th century. Ironically Wallace proved unworthy of the Shakers' trust in 1818 when he deserted the community and bilked members of $3,000. (Walter Havighurst Special Collections, Miami University Libraries.)

Francis Dunlavy was a framer of the Ohio constitution, Lebanon's first schoolmaster, a common pleas court judge, and an influential defender of the Shakers' rights in Warren County. His brother, John, was an important Shaker leader and author. A Dunlavy descendent, Gwendolyn Dunlavy Kelly, painted Francis's watercolor portrait on ivory. (Warren County Historical Society.)

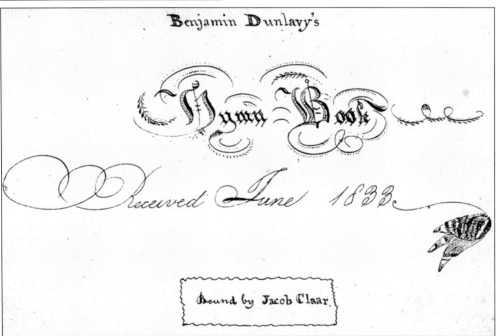

Benjamin Dunlavy's

Hymn Book

Received June 1833.

Bound by Jacob Claar

John Dunlavy's son Benjamin collected favorite songs in this beautifully lettered hymnal in 1833. Turtle Creek Shakers were the first in the sect to put words to their sacred vocal music in 1805. Many of the songs in Benjamin's book are attributed to his uncle, Richard McNemar, who became the sect's most prolific composer. Benjamin followed in his father's footsteps when he was named lead elder at Pleasant Hill, Kentucky. (Warren County Historical Society.)

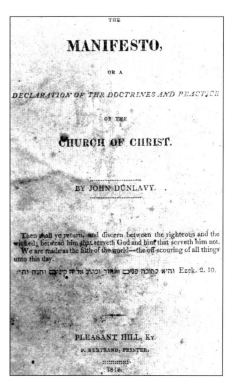

The Tree of Life

204

3 The tree of life is free for all Its fruit is sweet its branches

Under its shade I will retreat And when I'm faint its fruit I'll eat

O come ye nations far abroad And taste this fruit & serve the Lord

Its leaves will heal each wounded soul And set them free from sins control

Union Village. Oct. 1856.

2 When sorrows fill thy heart And afflictions have thy way I send my holy

"The tree of life is free for all. Its fruit is sweet, its branches tall," begins the Union Village song preserved in Benjamin's hymnal. The song is attributed to Union Village and may have been written by McNemar. The tree of life has become the most commonly recognized motifs of the Shaker faith. (Warren County Historical Society.)

The Manifesto is Elder John Dunlavy's best-known work and a classic of Shaker thought. John was McNemar's brother-in-law and also a Presbyterian until he joined dissenters led by McNemar. As McNemar gathered new Shakers at Turtle Creek, Dunlavy spread the Shaker message at Eagle Creek in present day Brown County. John eventually became the leading elder at Pleasant Hill, Kentucky. (Warren County Historical Society.)

THE

TESTIMONY

OF

CHRIST'S

SECOND APPEARING

CONTAINING

A GENERAL STATEMENT OF ALL THINGS

PERTAINING TO THE FAITH AND PRACTICE OF

THE CHURCH OF GOD

IN THIS LATTER-DAY

PUBLISHED IN UNION.

BY ORDER OF THE MINISTRY

Now is come salvation, and strength, and the kingdom of
our God and the power of his Christ.   REVELATION.

LEBANON, STATE OF OHIO :

FROM THE PRESS OF JOHN M'CLEAN

OFFICE OF THE WESTERN STAR

1808

Eldress Lucy Wright, Ann Lee's successor, hesitantly permitted the new Shaker settlement to publish *The Testimony of Christ's Second Appearing* in 1808. Wright correctly predicted that the Shakers' opponents would use the theology expressed in the book against them. Shakers believed that people could still receive divine revelations, meaning that the Bible was not God's final word. Opponents charged that the Shakers' wanted to substitute *The Testimony of Christ's Second Appearing* for the standard Bible. They derisively called the book the "Shaker Bible." Nonetheless Shakers closely studied and followed *The Testimony of Christ's Second Appearing* for many years. New Lebanon missionary Benjamin Youngs was the primary author although Elder David Darrow and missionary John Meacham also signed the first edition. Newspaper publisher John McClean printed the book in his Lebanon office. On the spine, the book is called *Shaking Quakers*, the name opponents gave Shakers in England. Ann Lee and her followers had been an offshoot of a Quaker sect there. Members shook and trembled with emotion as they worshipped, resulting in the nickname. (Warren County Historical Society.)

20

As Union Village's population grew during its first two decades, its Shaker craftsmen made more furnishings and household goods. Daniel Sering, one of the original Turtle Creek converts, could not resist signing a drawer back on this chest that he made in 1827. Sering was 13 when he joined with his family in 1805. He undoubtedly learned his craft from some of the older brothers. (Warren County Historical Society.)

Sering used walnut, butternut, and popular woods harvested from Union Village land to craft his 1827 chest of drawers. Shakers there sold some chairs, spinning wheels, and related items to the public, but most of the furniture made in the village was for the residents. The curved base of the piece may appear rather decorative to Shaker purists, but it is a common feature of Ohio Shaker furniture. (Warren County Historical Society.)

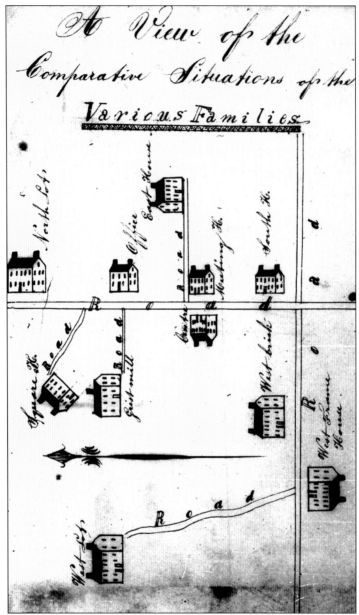

Like other Shaker communities, Union Village was composed of various families, groups of unrelated people who had become brothers and sisters in Christ. Each family had its own house, or dwelling, as well as various shops, barns, gardens, and fields. Men and women maintained separate quarters within the dwellings. This compressed view of the village shows the location of each family. The meetinghouse, office, and center house are in the heart of the village. The head elder and eldress, as well as their respective associates or seconds, lived upstairs in the meetinghouse. Shakers who were considered very firm and advanced in their faith lived in the center house. Trustees oversaw the village's industries from the trustees' office, where guests stayed during business or social visits. This sketch, and the ones on pages 23 and 24, were drawn by Shaker George Kendall in 1835. They are based on the original drawings made by Isaac N. Youngs, an elder from New Lebanon, during an 1834 visit. (Warren County Historical Society.)

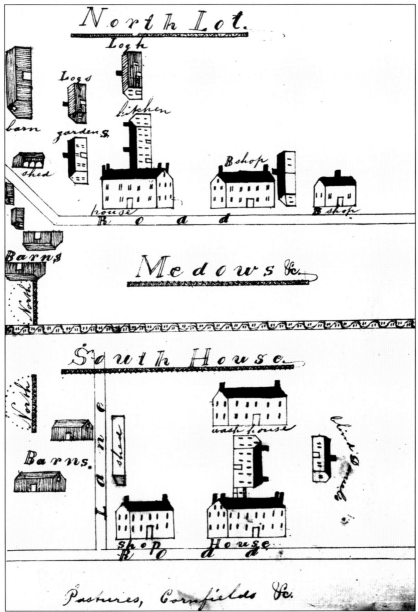

The North lot, or family, shown at the top of the drawing, includes a large dwelling with the kitchen wing at the rear, as was common at the time. Barns, sheds, and gardens are also indicated. The structures to the right of the dwelling are the brothers' shops that became the site of a successful brick and pottery business in 1836. By 1819, Shakers were manufacturing the first of millions of bricks used to construct their large dwellings, and by 1824, they were producing earthenware and pottery for the public, making Union Village the only known commercial Shaker pottery. At the South Family, shown at the bottom, a separate log cabin allowed Brother Daniel Stag to be independent, despite his blindness, and to keep a companion dog. Shakers accommodated members with special needs while keeping them as involved in their families as possible. The washhouse at the rear of the dwelling was the equivalent of a commercial laundry for the families. (Warren County Historical Society.).

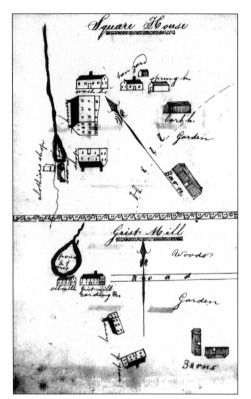

Most of Union Village's businesses began to serve residents and then expanded to the public, such as the gristmill and sawmill shown in this drawing. Members who were especially talented in a particular field were sent to various Shaker communities in the United States to share new ideas and techniques. This practice led to consistency in practices and products throughout the United Society and helped establish Shaker as a style name. (Warren County Historical Society.)

The dwelling at the East lot was the home for the village's children for many years. Children were raised together by several sisters, educated at the village school, and taught practical skills by their elders. Richard McNemar, the respected Shaker leader, originally owned the East lot property; his old cabin is shown behind the children's house. (Warren County Historical Society.)

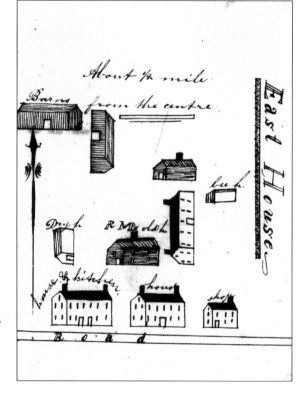

Two

A Big Farm

As a trustee for over 30 years, Peter Boyd transacted business between Union Village and the "world," as non-Shakers were called, as well as with other Shaker communities. Much of Boyd's work focused on agricultural products and livestock. He notified farmers when new stock was available, searched for particular herbs when the herbal medicine department ran short, sent brooms down to the New Orleans markets, and sought collection of bills past due. Boyd's image and signature were eventually used to advertise Union Village's most popular products. (Warren County Historical Society.)

25

This bucolic painting by an unknown local artist reflects the Shakers' importance as top livestock producers in Warren County. They were the first to import merino sheep from Spain to the region in 1812. Due to import restrictions, a full-blooded ram could cost as high as $2,500. Their success with the breed influenced other farmers to raise the animals for their luxurious fleece. (Warren County Historical Society.)

The Shakers' carding factory, long unused in this 1916 photograph, was once a vital part of Union Village's economy. In 1821, a total of 3,000 pounds of wool was carded. Production ebbed and flowed over the years but when demand for woolen goods increased with the Civil War, the Shakers built up their flock to 1,000, purchased knitting machines to increase productivity, and started building a new woolen mill. (Otterbein-Lebanon Archives.)

Union Village's most notable contribution to livestock history is the development of the Poland China hog. Shaker farmers developed the breed in 1816, helping to establish southwestern Ohio farmers as pork producers for the nation and Cincinnati as "Porkopolis." A monument to the Poland China hog breed was dedicated around 1900 on old U.S. Route 25 in Blue Ball, about five miles northwest of Union Village. (Warren County Historical Society.)

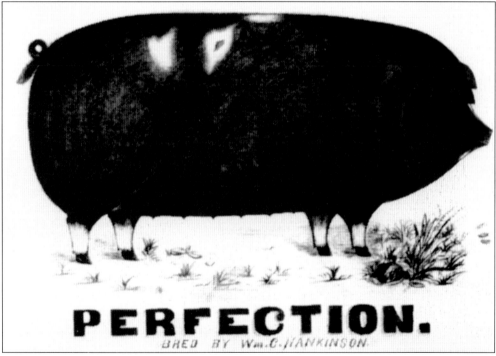

Bred by Warren County farmer William C. Hankinson, Perfection is an outstanding example of the kind of animal raised by the Shakers. Ironically, although the Shakers became renowned for developing and breeding the Poland Chinas, they prohibited pork consumption during various times of religious revival within the community. (Warren County Historical Society.)

When Otterbein took over the village, pork production resumed. This time, much of the pork was used to feed the local residents. These unidentified men inspect hogs at the West Frame Family lot in 1916. Otterbein people continued to use the Shaker names for the various buildings and areas of the village for several years after buying the property. (Otterbein-Lebanon Archives.)

This herd of dairy cattle at the West Frame Family farm produced milk, butter, and cheese for Otterbein residents in 1916. The Shakers had maintained large herds to feed their members and also to sell to the public. They were importing cattle from England and Scotland by 1817. Cattle became another valuable part of their farm economy, and they shipped stock to several states. (Otterbein-Lebanon Archives.)

Following the Shakers' practice of training youngsters in varied tasks, Otterbein's children also helped with daily chores. In this c. 1916 photograph, the "milk brigade" files into the Center Family barn for evening milking. A tenant farmer follows the boys. The Shakers began renting out land to tenant farmers in 1841, and Otterbein Home officials continued the tradition. (Otterbein-Lebanon Archives.)

The number of barns at the West Family lot in 1916 attests to the Shakers' success in agriculture. Brother John Meacham, one of first Shaker missionaries to visit Turtle Creek, proved to be an accurate observer when he wrote in 1805, "The face of the country . . . is in the main very beautiful . . . and as for the depth and richness of soil, it far exceeds any country we ever saw before." (Otterbein-Lebanon Archives.)

The dairy barn at the Center Family housed 60 cows when this picture was taken in 1916. The barn was one of 60 original Shaker structures still standing when Otterbein purchased the property in 1912. Today three Shaker buildings remain on Otterbein property. (Otterbein-Lebanon Archives.)

One of the most industrious families in the village, the North Family was also active in farming. This building is one of five barns and sheds that once served the family. This photograph was taken in 1916, when the barn had not been used for many years. (Otterbein-Lebanon Archives.)

This Shaker-designed winnowing machine could be used to clean seed or separate grain from chaff. Necessity was the mother of many Shaker innovations during the 19th century. (Otterbein-Lebanon Archives.)

<table>
<tr><td colspan="2">

Memorandum.

Town. _Celina_

Name. _W Schmidt & Bro_

Rec'd ..... box, ... papers.

Net Price per paper **5** cents.

Am't Packages Rec'd $

Ret'd ..... box , ... papers.

Am't Packages Ret'd $

Amount paid $

</td><td>

Dayton March 16 **187 5**

Received of the SHAKERS OF UNION VILLAGE, OHIO, _for sale,_ ..1.. box containing _150.._ papers of SHAKER GARDEN SEEDS, to be retailed at not less than **8** cents per paper. The undersigned hereby promise to pay, or to direct successor to pay **5** cents per paper, and 75 cents per box, for all not returned in good order, to the bearer. Also received a lot of Seeds in larger Packages, amounting to $ _2.50_ , all sold to be accounted for at prices marked on them, less 25   per cent commission.

Knersly & Wr Latine

</td></tr>
</table>

Shaker seed salesmen traveled from the Great Lakes to the Deep South to peddle their wares. This 1875 receipt was written closer to home in Dayton. Another Shaker community, Watervliet, existed near Dayton and also produced seeds for a regional market. The Shakers not only raised and harvested the seeds, they also built the boxes that held the seed packets, or papers, and printed the packets. (Warren County Historical Society.)

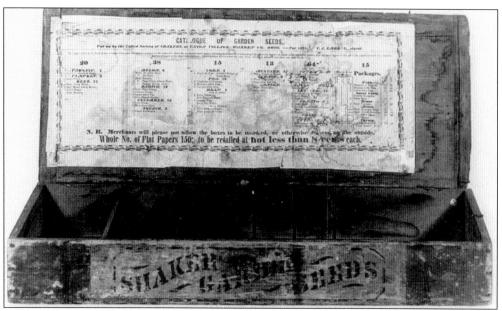

Very few seed boxes with printed labels survive from Union Village. This box from 1875 still contains a label listing the seed selection for that season. Shaker brothers took boxes such as this on their sales routes to leave with shopkeepers in the Midwest and South. The Shakers of Union Village were the first people to package seeds in the small paper packets that modern gardeners still use. (Warren County Historical Society.)

IT IS A FACT,

Well known, that the general character of the Extract of Sarsaparilla, now in market, is deficient in quality. The truth is, a perfect article costs more than can be afforded for the price at which it is generally sold; therefore, we would say to the public, and will appeal to the medical profession for the TRUTH OF THE STATEMENT, that wherever a quart bottle of "SAID TO BE" Sarsaparilla Extract is offered for One Dollar, it is utterly deficient in quality, and can not be a true and legitimate article.

To prevent imposition we have procured a mould for our bottles, lettered as follows: "SHAKER SARSAPARILLA, prepared by the United Society, at Union Village, Ohio, P. BOYD, Agent.

All prepared at Union Village bears the *fac simile* signature of

Peter Boyd

Sarsaparilla syrup and extract became one of Union Village's most prominent and profitable products. Sarsaparilla was touted as a tonic for everything from skin diseases to arthritis. The Shaker brand became so popular that imitators began labeling their products as Shaker, leading Trustee Peter Boyd to manufacture a special bottle bearing Union Village's name and his signature. (Warren County Historical Society.)

If you would have a Clear Complexion, smooth and soft, try

SHAKER

SARSAPARILLA.

Has been on the market for over THIRTY *years.*
Manufactured by the United Society at Union V...

GRAHAM BROTHERS,

Wholesale Agents.

For Sale by All Druggists.

The Graham Brothers published this advertising brochure in 1889 to promote Union Village sarsaparilla and herbal medicines. Shaker products were known for purity and quality. Advertisements from this era frequently carried the Lebanon Medical Society's endorsement that had been made in the 1850s. Union Village was among the top four Shaker producers of herbal medicines by the mid-19th century. They grew dozens of plants, producing medicines, extracts, and essential oils that were sold nationally and aboard. When supplies fell short, they purchased herbs from other Shaker communities. America's first Shakers had learned about many indigenous herbal remedies from Native Americans in New York State in the late 1700s. Union Village Shakers gained more knowledge when they befriended a Shawnee community in Darke County in 1807. (Warren County Historical Society.)

SHAKER
Cough Syrup

This medicine is precisely what its name imports, and has been in use for a number of years among the several families of the Society of Shakers, as the principal remedy for Coughs and affections of the Chest.

It is a Tonic Anodyne expectorant; and being prepared expressly for domestic use, the choicest of ingredients have been selected; these have been prepared and combined by the most approved chemical processes, without regard to labor or expense.

☞ This is not a **Patent Medicine,** nor a Secret Remedy, and we make no secret of its composition.

The **Basis** of this preparation is fresh **Wild Cherry Bark.** The efficacy of Wild Cherry in Pectoral affections is universally known; but the object is frequently defeated by a want of skill or knowledge in the preparation. The Organic Acid to which it owes its peculiar virtues, is very volatile, and consequently is destroyed or dissipated by heat; hence the disappointment so often experienced in the use of this invaluable remedy. From ignorance or carelessness the Bark is kept until every particle of the Aromatic Acid has evaporated; or it is subjected to the temperature of boiling alcohol or water, by which all its medicinal virtues are scattered to the winds.

In our preparation the bark used is fresh, and the Extract is made with cold Alcohol—the powerful and agreeable Aroma of the Wild Cherry is there to speak for itself.

Besides the Wild Cherry, Squills and Seneca Snake-root are the leading ingredients of the Shaker Cough Syrup.

Rhubarb is also added. This is, perhaps, a novel ingredient in a cough mixture, but we are satisfied of its value, from long experience. It acts as a mild tonic, and is also useful in preventing constipation and regulating the action of the bowels, thus obviating the common necessity of resorting to the use of cathartic medicines.

Morphia and Antimony, in very small proportions, are the remaining constituents. Notwithstanding the prejudices of ignorance, physicians know the value of opium and antimony in pectoral affections. The one allays irritation, the other acts as a sedative, expectorant and febrifuge; in combination they meet many indications in diseases of the respiratory organs, better than almost any other medicament; and when united with the other ingredients of this preparation, they complete, as we verily believe, the best Cough Medicine ever offered to the afflicted.

Persons desiring the Cough Syrup can be supplied by addressing

For Sale by Druggists Generally.

Cough syrup was another signature product of Union Village. The Shakers believed that by educating the public about the ingredients of their medicine, they could differentiate themselves from patent medicine salesmen, whose tonics were often worthless. Having been the first to widely sell herbal medicines, the Shakers continued to tweak their preparations in the face of competitors. Rhubarb was the special ingredient in their cough syrup. (Dr. M. Stephen and Miriam R. Miller.)

CATALOGUE OF
MEDICAL PLANTS, EXTRACTS,
ESSENTIAL OILS, ETC.

PREPARED AND FOR SALE BY

THE UNITED SOCIETY OF SHAKERS, AT UNION VILLAGE, O.

Our Herbs are put up in Half-pound, Quarter-pound, and Ounce packages; Roots and Barks in One pound. A discount of 25 per cent. to regular retail customers, and will be raised in proportion to amount purchased by wholesale dealers. In this we hope to give full satisfaction. ☞An additional charge of 8 cents net per pound will be made for ounce packages. ☞No extra charge for half and quarter pound packages of Roots and Barks.

TERMS CASH.

Herbs, Roots, and Barks, with their Common and Botanical Names.

	Per Lb.			Per Lb.
Aconite leaves......Aconitum napellus........	$0 40		Blue Flag root......Iris versicolor..............	30
Aconite root.......... '' ''	40		Blue Vervain......Verbene hastata............	20
American hellebore......Veratrim viride....	50		Boneset herb......Eupatorium perfoliatum..	25
Agrimony......Agrimonia eupatoria........ ...	35		Borage, or Bugloss......Borago officinalis.....	30
Angelica......Angelica atropurprea..........	40		Box-wood bark......Cornus Florida............	20
Apple-tree bark......... Pirus malus.............	40		Burdock leaves......Arctium lappa.............	20
Balm Gilead buds...Populus balsamifera....	1 00		'' root...... '' ''	25
Balmony......Chelone glabra................	35		'' seed...... '' ''	30
Barberry bark......Berberis vulgaris..........	40		Black Hellebore......Helleborus Niger........	50
Barberry leaves ..... '' ''			Butternut bark......Juglans cineria...........	20
Bayberry.,....Myrica cerifera...............	35		Button Snake-root......Liatris spicata.........	35
Bearberry......Arbutus uva ursi.......	25		Calamus......Acorus calamus............	30
Beech drop......Orobanche virginiana........	25		Canada Snake-root......Asarum canadense...	40
Beech leaves .....Fagus feruginea...............	20		Cancer Root .....Orobanche virginiana.......	25
Benne leaves .....Sesamum orientale..........	30		Caraway seed......Carum carui............:....	30
Beth Root......Trillium pendulum..............	35		Carpenter's Square......Scrophularia mari-	
Bitter Bugle......Lycopus vulgaris..........	30		landica	25
Bitter Root.....Apocynum androsæmifolium	30		Catnep......Nepeta cataria.............	25
Bitter Sweet......Solanum dulcamara........	35		Cicuta leaves......Conium maculatum........	20
Black Alder......Prinos verticillatus..........	25		Cleavers......Galium aparine...............	25
Blackberry root......Rubus villosus.............	25		Colt's-foot herb......Tussilago farfara.......	. 45
Black Birch bark......Betula lenta.............	25		Comfrey......Symphytum officinalis...........	30
Black Indian Hemp Apocynum cannabinum	40		Coriander seed......Cariandrum sativum.....	25
Black Mustard Seed......Sinapis nigra........	25		Cow-parsnep leaves......Heracleum lanatum	30
Black Oak bark......Quercus tinctoria........	20		'' root......... '' ''	40
Black Root......Leptandra vir inica	35		'' seed......... '' ''	50
Black Snake-root......Macrotys racemosa.....	25		Cramp bark......Virburnum opulus...........	30
Blessed Thistle......Centaurea benedicta......	30		Crane's Bill......Geranium maculatum........	30
Blood Root .....Sanguinaria canensis........	25		Culver's root......Leptandra virginica.........	30
Blue Cohosh......Cauloph'lum thalictroides	25		Dandelion leaves......Leontodon taraxacum..	25

This is the first page of a four-page catalogue of herbal medicines from the 1850s, which hints at the extent of Union Village's herb industry. During the peak years in the 1840s and 1850s, the herb industry averaged $150,000 in annual sales. The Shakers operated a laboratory in the rear of the trustees' office, where they prepared extracts and oils using sophisticated technology for the time. This catalogue lists the price per pound and gives incentives to wholesalers to purchase larger quantities. Cancer root is one of the intriguing items listed. Recipes for cancer cures have been found in old Shaker notebooks. (Dr. M. Stephen and Miriam R. Miller.)

Shakers turned briefly to commercial wine making in the 1890s in an unsuccessful attempt to bolster revenues. The label identifies them as Shaker communists, referring to their communal lifestyle. Most members were teetotalers by that time, but in earlier years, they had produced a variety of medicinal wines for the community and sold their grapes to Cincinnati's Nicholas Longworth, who was the first to market Ohio wines. (Warren County Historical Society.)

The return address on this 1897 envelope illustrates Union Village's efforts to become identified with the wine industry. The Wickliffe vineyards mentioned were in Lake County in northeastern Ohio. The North Union Shaker community near Cleveland had operated orchards and a vineyard at Wickliffe since the late 1870s. When North Union closed in 1899, the Shakers retained the Wickliffe property. (Dr. M. Stephen and Miriam R. Miller.)

SHAKER VINEYARD
GRAPES

Dear Sir: — We are planning now to handle what is probably the largest crop of grapes ever raised in an American vineyard — that of the United Society of Shakers at Wickliffe, Ohio.

As far as the efforts of the producers can go, we intend the distribution of this crop to be in proportion to its importance in size. That is to say, in the selection of the best grapes in our vineyard, the careful picking of the same, the sorting at the packing house, and the loading direct from the packing house to the car without the jolting of express wagons, and above all in the loading of solid cars of one variety of grapes from one vineyard and all one style of packing, we are accomplishing something which you as a handler of grapes must know the significance of. While we have no desire to detract from the merits of the "Association Plan" of marketing grapes from smaller vineyards, and in fact believe that it is the best plan yet conceived for smaller growers, we do desire to bring to your notice the immense advantage of our plan to the carload dealers and to smaller dealers and consumers.

For instance, you are perhaps a retail dealer or a shipper of grapes. You have bought a car of grapes of one of the numerous Associations in Ohio or New York. You unload your first car. The first wagon load is choice fruit packed in a choice manner and very satisfactory. The next is similar. You sell the two loads out quickly to good advantage. Possibly your first customer calls you over the "phone" and orders all the balance of the grapes in the car for his next day's trade and on the strength of this trade you order another and perhaps two more cars of the Association. You go home that night feeling that your grape trade is booming and that the Association. Plan is the right one. The next morning a different state of affairs shows up. Your telephone bell rings and your big customer of yesterday wants to know "what is the matter with the other grapes in that car." You try to put on a bold front and say they are "the same," etc., but he silences you quickly by saying "come and see." You know what this means, so to save time you say "send them back." They come and you see that your customer is justified in his rejection, as the balance of the car are of an entirely different packing and a different appearing grape although the same variety. You wire the Association to cancel your order for the two cars but you are too late. They have already started so you have the same troubles and others probably to go through with on these.

Now please consider the difference if you trade with us. We shall load probably FROM TWO TO FOUR CARS PER DAY OF ONE VARIETY OF GRAPES PACKED BY THE SAME HANDS AND FROM THE SAME VINEYARD. This insures perfect uniformity of packing. It also insures fresh receipts as we do not believe in the Association Plan of holding grapes on track waiting for an improvement in the market. We believe in marketing our grapes when they are ripe regardless of market conditions.

We shall greatly appreciate any trade you see fit to give us this year and are confident that our well earned reputation for fair dealing in all matters will make a permanent customer of you for our grapes. Please correspond with F. Newhall & Sons, 125 South Water Street, Chicago, who will attend to the Western distribution, or direct with our Society here. Respectfully, etc.

THE UNITED SOCIETY OF SHAKERS,

Union Village, Ohio, ———————— 1897.   WM. C. AYER, Asst. Trustee.

This rare 1897 broadsheet advertisement invokes the Shaker reputation for quality to entice wholesalers. Whether the Shakers were selling seeds, herbal medicine, or wine, they stressed the freshness and wholesomeness of their products. The advertisement also differentiates between Shaker business practices and those of the world. While other producers might hold onto their grapes waiting for a price increase, the Shakers pledged to sell their grapes at the height of freshness, regardless of price. Trustee William C. Ayer's name appears in the right bottom corner. Union Village records of the period chronicle numerous trips by Ayer and Elder Joseph Slingerland to the Wickliffe "grape farm." Union Village had a telegraph line installed to facilitate communication with Wickliffe and prospective wholesalers. Ayer also secured an agent in Chicago who was to handle orders from the West. The plan never succeeded as hoped, however, and by 1900 Union Village was out of the grape business. (Dr. M. Stephen and Miriam R. Miller.)

This display at the Warren County Historical Society in Lebanon shows the equipment used in making brooms, another major Union Village industry. The Shakers raised their own broomcorn to turn out brooms ranging from a few inches to feet. Cleanliness and order were vital to the Shaker life, and through their broom business, they passed those ideals on to the public. (Warren County Historical Society.)

Union Village's broom factory, built by the Shakers from bricks that they fired, was heavily used for most of the 19th century. Brooms made by the North Family brothers were sold from the Great Lakes to the Gulf of Mexico. When the Civil War threatened to destroy the Shakers' economy at South Union, Kentucky, Union Village sent hundreds of brooms to be sold to the public. (Otterbein-Lebanon Archives.)

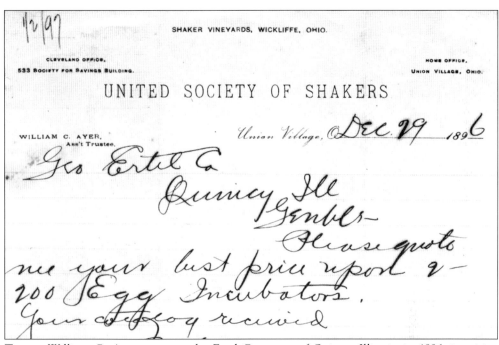

Geo Ertel Co
Quincy Ill
Genbles —
Please quote
me your best price upon 9 —
200 Egg Incubators.
Your catalog received

Trustee William C. Ayer wrote to the Ertel Company of Quincy, Illinois, in 1896, inquiring about egg incubators. Although the Shakers had given up commercial livestock production by that time, they continued to raise their own poultry. The letterhead lists three addresses: the Wickliffe vineyards, a business office in Cleveland, and the home office at Union Village. (Dr. M. Stephen and Miriam R. Miller.)

The gristmill was one of the first Shaker endeavors opened to the public by the 1820s. Commerce between the Shakers and the world helped familiarize the public with members of the sect and fostered tolerance among previous opponents. The Shakers came to be respected for their integrity and work ethic. This photograph shows the mill, no longer in use, in August 1919. (Dr. C. Nelson Melampy.)

In this 1916 photograph, a farmer operates the tractor and binder, while an Otterbein official watches. Barns of the West Family can be seen in the background. Shakers were enthusiastic about new technology that saved time and labor such as the tractor and car in this picture. They purchased a new car shortly before the village disbanded in 1912. (Otterbein-Lebanon Archives.)

Boys from the Otterbein Home helped transfer hay from field to barn in this 1917 photograph. Mules and horses were still widely used on the farm at the time, making this scene reminiscent of Shaker days. (Otterbein-Lebanon Archives.)

Tenant farmers bring in the hay crop at the Center Family farm in this 1916 photograph. (Otterbein-Lebanon Archives.)

Philip Tillman's home at the West Family farm is shown in this 1916 picture. Tillman was one of several tenant farmers for the Shakers and later for Otterbein. The Shakers began leasing land and livestock to tenants in 1841. Some of the tenants lived within the village in buildings that had once been Shaker shops. (Otterbein-Lebanon Archives.)

Children of the Otterbein Home work in their own garden plots in this 1916 photograph. Almost everyone had a home garden at the time and teaching children how to garden was part of raising them to be self-sufficient adults. Shaker children had also helped adults garden and assisted in the seed shops during the busy seasons. (Otterbein-Lebanon Archives.)

The cattle barn at the South Family attests to the large herds the Shakers once had. Many of the South Family's buildings were destroyed in an 1890 fire that proved to be arson. (Otterbein-Lebanon Archives.)

Three

COMMUNITY LIFE

Sisters work in luxury in the kitchen of the remodeled trustees' office in this 1913 photograph. Surrounded by walnut woodwork and marble floors, the sisters canned produce from their garden, baked bread, and cooked meals for their family. Seen here are, from left to right, Lucy Hunt, Jennie H. Fish, Eldress Clymena Miner, Harriet Drought, and Aida Elam. Elder Joseph Slingerland spearheaded the elaborate remodeling in 1891–1892 in an unsuccessful attempt to attract new members. (Otterbein-Lebanon Archives.)

TABLE MONITOR.

GATHER UP THE FRAGMENTS THAT REMAIN, THAT NOTHING BE LOST.—Christ.

Here then is the pattern
  Which Jesus has set ;
And his good example
  We cannot forget :
With thanks for his blessings
  His word we'll obey ;
But on this occasion
  We've somewhat to say.

We wish to speak plainly
  And use no deceit ;
We like to see fragments
  Left wholesome and neat :
To customs and fashions
  We make no pretence ;
Yet think we can tell
  What belongs to good sense.

What we deem good order,
  We're willing to state—
Eat hearty and decent,
  And clear out our plate—
Be thankful to Heaven
  For what we receive,
And not make a mixture
  Or compound to leave.

We find of those bounties
  Which heaven doth give,
That some live to eat,
  And, that some eat to live—
That some think of nothing
  But pleasing the taste,
And care very little
  How much they do waste.

Tho' Heaven has bless'd us
  With plenty of food :
Bread, butter and honey
  And all that is good ;
We lothe to see mixtures
  Where gentle folks dine,
Which scarcely look fit
  For the poultry or swine.

We find often left,
  On the same china dish,
Meat, applesauce, pickle,
  Brown bread and minc'd fish ;
Another's replenish'd
  With butter and cheese ;
With pie, cake and toast,
  Perhaps, added to these.

Now if any virtue
  In this can be shown,
By peasant, by lawyer,
  Or king on the throne,
We freely will forfeit
  Whatever we've said,
And call it a virtue
  To waste meat and bread.

Let none be offended
  At what we here say ;
We candidly ask you,
  Is that the best way ?
If not,—lay such customs
  And fashions aside,
And take this monitor
  Henceforth for your guide.

Shaker Home, 1830

The "Table Monitor" poem, widely referred to in many Shaker communities, advises diners about table manners and admonishes those who would waste food. By 1830 when this verse was written, Union Village was a prosperous community where members enjoyed comfortable homes, steady work, free education, and plenty of wholesome food. During bad economic times and periods of personal crisis, many homeless people came to live at Union Village temporarily. The Shakers accepted anyone who seemed sincere and was willing to live by the sect's rules. Some of these people became Shakers; many of them, however, moved on when the times and their personal circumstances improved. (Warren County Historical Society.)

The First (or Center) Family of Union Village lived in this dwelling in the heart of the village on the east side of State Route 741. Members of this family were considered the most spiritually advanced and firmest in their faith. The porches visible in this 1948 photograph were added by Otterbein officials, who called the dwelling Old Bethany Hall. (Otterbein-Lebanon Archives.)

One of the earliest photographs of the Center Family dwelling appeared in *Warren County Illustrated*, a book published by Lebanon photographer A. G. Gilmore around 1902. In this photograph, the dwelling does not have any porches, State Route 741 is still a dirt road, and the Shakers' meetinghouse is visible in the distance. (Otterbein-Lebanon Archives.)

Anna and Max Goepper Jr. of Morrow sat for this *c.* 1876 photograph shortly before they moved with their family to Union Village. They followed their uncle, Leopold Goepper, who had left his wife, Belle Goepper, to raise the couple's eight children on a Morrow area farm. Like Leopold, Anna became interested in spiritualism. Max left the Shakers at 16 to seek his fortune in the world. (Otterbein-Lebanon Archives.)

A group of Union Village's last Shakers was photographed in 1913. Seen here are, from left to right, James Fennessey, Eldress Clymena Miner, the adult Anna Goepper, Moore Mason, and an unidentified man. Goepper's religious writings are preserved at the Watervliet, New York, Shaker site. (Otterbein-Lebanon Archives.)

GOOD WILL TO ALL.

O. C. HAMPTON.

The goodness of God leadeth on to repentance;
  Forgiveness, the need of confession sincere;
Man's weakness, a plea for entire dependence
  On God's tender mercies while traveling here.

Contrition and sorrow become the Believer,
  For sin and short coming, and hardness of heart;
And who of such gift is the happy receiver
  Can truly be said to possess the "good part."

I know that the true consecration of spirit
  Which we are commanded in deed to possess,
Is genuine Love and good will to inherit,
  And ev'ry good saint and vile sinner to bless.

To soften each feeling of coldness and hardness
  In tender conpassion, to friend and to foe;
Of all to be anxious and watchful, regardless
  Of what they are doing or going to do.

The old roots of bitterness, malice and slander,
  O let us dig up, and consume in the fire
Of patient forgiveness, and charity tender,
  If nearer to Heaven and Christ we aspire.

Cease, once and forever, from all evil speaking,
  And learn the new language, to speak well of all;
The good and the union of all to be seeking,
  For this is in earnest the trumpet's loud call.

Why should we continue to injure each other
  O God! shall the sword never cease to devour?
O are we not ready, dear Sister and Brother,
  Of Peaceful *at-one-ment*, to hail the glad hour?

Sweet union, is Heaven on earth to believers
  It strengthens the wav'ring, and comforts the strong;
Ev'n here in this life, from all grief it delivers,
  And fits us for joys of Eternity long.
    Union Village, Ohio.

Elder Oliver Hampton wrote about the fundamental Shaker precepts of repentance, forgiveness, charity, and harmony in the March 1882 issue of the *Shaker Manifesto*, a monthly publication of the United Society of Believers. A schoolmaster, author, public speaker, and leader, Hampton was one of Union Village's most influential members during the last half of the 19th century. He sought to bridge the religious gap between the Shakers and their worldly neighbors by writing in community newspapers and speaking at public venues outside the village. (Warren County Historical Society.)

A tailor by vocation, Harvey Lauderdale Eades lived at Union Village from 1844 to 1862, publishing the *Tailor's Division System*, his own system to train other tailors. During the Civil War, Eades was sent to South Union, Kentucky, where he served as an elder and important theologian. Shakers believe that even their top spiritual leaders should also work in skilled jobs. (Warren County Historical Society.)

Eades's collection of sermons went through several editions and helped make him one of the most highly regarded Shaker thinkers of the latter half of the 19th century. The volume shown here was a gift presented to Eades' friend, Eldress Emily Robinson of Union Village. Shakers from various villages often visited each other as well as exchanging gifts and correspondence through the mail. (Warren County Historical Society.)

SHAKER SERMONS:

SCRIPTO-RATIONAL.

CONTAINING THE SUBSTANCE OF

SHAKER THEOLOGY.

TOGETHER WITH

REPLIES AND CRITICISMS

LOGICALLY AND CLEARLY SET FORTH.

BY

H. L. EADS,

BISHOP OF SOUTH UNION, KY.

"The Supreme good in the mind is the knowledge of God, and the highest virtue of the mind is to know God." —SPINOZA.

"There is no soul so feeble but that, well directed, it may attain to absolute control over the [animal] passions."—DESCARTES.

"And this is life eternal, that they might know Thee the only true God and Jesus Christ whom Thou hast sent."—CHRIST.

FIFTH EDITION.
REVISED AND ENLARGED.

SOUTH UNION, KENTUCKY.
1889.

Emily Robinson was born to Michael and Mary Robinson of Hamilton County around 1838. The 1850 census lists her at Union Village. She was named as first eldress of the community in the 1880 census, around the time this image was made. Robinson remained a Shaker until her death, approximately 16 years later. Eades's book was among her possessions. (Warren County Historical Society.)

Eades autographed his book of sermons for Robinson "with kindest regards" around 1890, noting that he was "now fair in his 84th year." (Warren County Historical Society.)

49

Heavenly Flight

I will take my flight from the dark shades of night I will soar to the regions of love Where the weary can rest with the happy & blest In the heavenly Mansions above. I will go on my way on my harp I will play the sweet songs of angelic myrth I will shout I will sing for the Lord he is king. And ruler in Heaven and Earth

U.V. Oct. 1846.

Song was an integral part of Shaker life. Richard McNemar of Union Village is said to have composed more hymns and songs than any other single Shaker. "Heavenly Flight," copied in the songbook of Pleasant Hill's Benjamin Dunlavy, is attributed to Union Village, 1846. The song speaks of taking refuge in God's love. (Warren County Historical Society.)

FORM A 93.

Investigator's Application.

Name .... Town .... State ....
Born .... Town .... State .... Parents' Address ....
.... Married? .... Single? .... Widow ? .... Brothers? ....
Sisters? .... If separated from your wife or husband is separation legal? ....
Children? .... Is anybody dependent on you for support? .... Can you liquidate all
your debts? .... Do you use tobacco? .... Do you use intoxicating liquors? ....
In moderation or excess? .... Present occupation .... Name of employer
.... Have you had experience in any other business pursuits? Enumerate

Talents and accomplishments ....

Have you ever lived in any other community? .... Name and address ....
.... Condition of health, past and present, also if troubled with chronic or acute
diseases, malformed or injured, full particulars ....

Religious faith if any? .... Your object in addressing us

Remarks ....

References, Name and Address ....
" " " " ....
" " " " ....

Children are accepted with parents. Fill out and return this preliminary application and we will be pleased to give you further particulars.

United Society of Believers,

Union Village, Ohio.

Interested parties had to fill out this investigator's application in the latter part of the 19th century. Because of early experiences with quarreling spouses and disgruntled heirs, the Shakers now tried to ascertain that prospective members were free to act on their own and that any specific problems were identified up front. (Warren County Historical Society.)

Sister Matilda A. Butler served as the first postmaster of the Union Village post office when it opened in July 1882. It was first called simply the Shaker post office, but took on the community's name in 1885. Five Shakers took turns operating the post office before it closed in May 1901. (Otterbein-Lebanon Archives.)

Shaker diarist Oliver Hampton wrote that Union Village's train depot was a "most beautiful little station" when it opened in 1892. The station was used primarily for shipping and receiving goods. It was still in use by Otterbein when this photograph was taken in 1916. (Otterbein-Lebanon Archives.)

At 51, Brother George Baxter (left) was the youngest Shaker living at Union Village when it was sold to the United Brethren Church in 1912. Baxter poses in this c. 1918 photograph with Shaker trustee James Fennessey. (Otterbein-Lebanon Archives.)

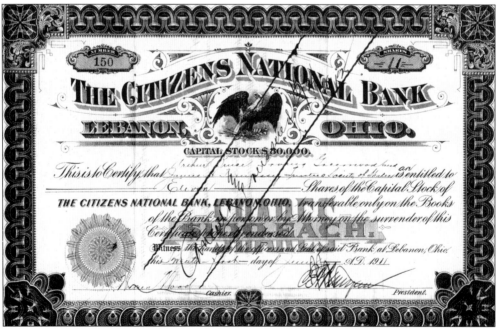

The Union Village Shakers invested in $30,000 of stock in the Lebanon Citizens National Bank in 1911 as part of an effort to straighten out their financial situation after a disastrous series of questionable investments by an elder in the 1890s. Fennessey, the village's last trustee, spent years clearing up the community's financial affairs. (Otterbein-Lebanon Archives.)

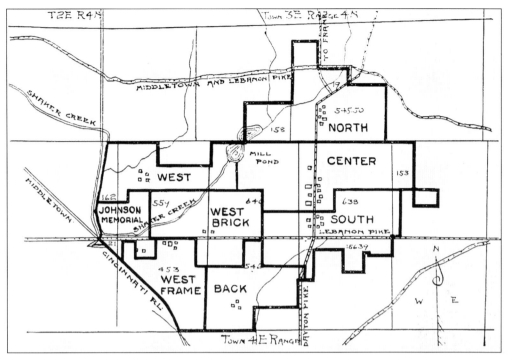

This drawing shows the layout of the village when the United Brethren Church purchased it in 1912. Otterbein managed 750 acres of farmland at the Center Family and 500 acres at the West Brick Family. The other land was leased to local farmers. (Otterbein-Lebanon Archives.)

The West Frame Family dwelling is shown in this 1916 photograph. Otterbein employees lived in this house for a while, but the structure, like many of the old frame buildings, did not survive long as Otterbein sought to provide shelter for a growing number of elderly people and children. (Otterbein-Lebanon Archives.)

Picture rails replace peg rails in this 1913 photograph of the parlor at the trustees' office. Although men and women always lived separately within their dwellings at Union Village, times were provided for them to socialize together as a group. Seen here are, from left to right, Harriet Drought, Lucy Hunt, Jennie H. Fish, Eldress Clymena Miner, Moore S. Mason, James Fennessey, and Aida Elam. Fewer than 20 Shakers remained at Union Village at this time. At the community's peak, more than 600 Shakers lived in the village. (Otterbein-Lebanon Archives.)

A tenant farmer named Harris farmed this western section after Otterbein's establishment. Farming remained an important part of the local economy and provided many jobs for hired hands. Dr. C. Nelson Melampy, whose father and grandfather farmed at Union Village, remembers hearing how his grandfather and siblings as children took a horse and buggy from nearby Monroe to Union Village to do chores for the Shakers. (Otterbein-Lebanon Archives.)

This peaceful scene is the location of one of Union Village's two burying grounds. Shakers do not believe in large monuments, so little remains at the site off State Route 741, which was sold by Otterbein to Armco Steel to use as an employees' park. The other burying ground, established in 1806, was part of the South Family lot. (Otterbein-Lebanon Archives.)

This early cherry bed and trundle may have been used at the East Family dwelling where a group of sisters lived with the community's children through the late 1830s. As the population boomed through the 1820s, Shaker furniture makers often had to produce a considerable amount of furniture quickly, training helpers as they worked. (Otterbein-Lebanon Archives.)

This wall of walnut doors and built-ins in a trustees' office room display the symmetry and simplicity for which Shaker design has become known. The built-in may date from the original 1810 structure; the closet doors are consistent with other woodwork installed as part of the trustees' office's renovation in the 1890s. (Otterbein-Lebanon Archives.)

This two-story frame house was moved from the South Family lot to the lawn between the trustees' office and New Bethany in 1918. Renamed Sunbeam Cottage, it served as an annex for young girls who lived at Otterbein. The cottage was razed in 1961. (Otterbein-Lebanon Archives.)

Several frame structures are visible on the grounds adjacent to the North Family dwelling in this c. 1916 photograph. Shakers were practical and frugal, often moving buildings to new sites or retooling an old structure to serve a new need. (Otterbein-Lebanon Archives.)

Shaker brothers James Fennessey and Moore S. Mason pose in their room in the remodeled trustees' office in 1913. They were among the last brothers to live at Union Village. Their room looks more Edwardian than Shaker, but the colorful carpet, fresh flowers, and abundant reading material attest to the comfortable lives the men enjoyed. Fennessey joined the Shakers in 1882 after a life of hardship. He eventually became the village's last trustee and was instrumental in negotiations between the United Society of Believers and the United Brethren Church after the decision was made to close the village. Mason left the Shakers in 1918 and died in 1922 in Cincinnati. The San Antonio pendant visible in the sleeping alcove now hangs in the archives office of the same building. (Otterbein-Lebanon Archives.)

Four

ORIGINS AND OFFSPRING

Shakerism began in England with Ann Lee who brought a small band of Shakers to America in 1774. Aided by fellow believer James Whittaker, Lee developed a faith that emphasized divine revelations, public confession of sins, and celibacy. Shaker communities developed over the last quarter of the 18th century in New York State and throughout New England. In 1805, Shaker missionaries traveled west of the Allegheny Mountains to spread their faith. In Warren County, the missionaries met with members of Richard McNemar's congregation who had broken away from the Presbyterian Church. That group became the nucleus of Union Village. This image of Ann Lee, James Whittaker (upper right), Jesus Christ (lower left), and St. Peter is part of a c. 1845 drawing by Sister Polly Collins entitled "Emblem of the Heavenly Sphere." (Andrews Collection, Hancock Shaker Village.)

The first Shaker missionaries to Warren County departed from Mount Lebanon, New York, on January 1, 1805. In the 1780s, Ann Lee predicated a religious revival in the Southwest. At that time, it included what would become Ohio, Indiana, and Kentucky. Mount Lebanon was the headquarters, or central ministry, for the United Society of Believers. Union Village became the headquarters or bishopric for all western Shaker communities. (Author's collection.)

Mount Lebanon was a large, thriving community by the time conversions began in Ohio. Agriculture, represented by the remains of a huge, five-story barn, was an important part of Mount Lebanon's economy. Leaders there hoped that agriculture would become even more lucrative for the Ohio Shakers. Missionary Joseph Meacham predicted in 1806 that Union Village would become wealthy if members followed Shaker precepts. (Author's collection.)

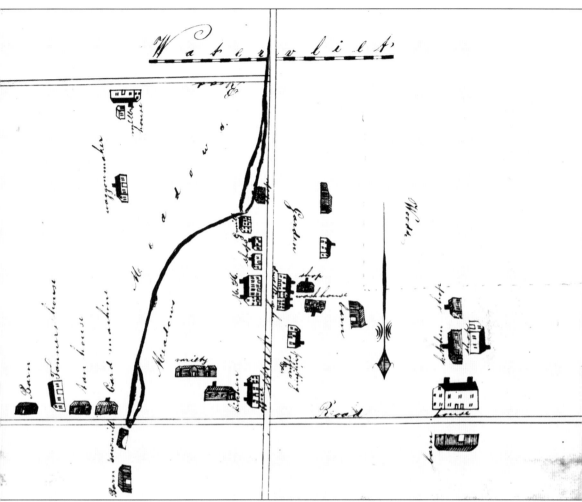

Watervliet was one of the first communities founded by the Union Village converts and Shaker missionaries. Although Watervliet never grew as large as its parent, approximately 125 people lived there between 1806 and 1900. Much of the community's 800 acres were devoted to agriculture and raising sheep. Watervliet's woolen mill produced textiles for the Shakers' use and for sale to the public. Members there also composed many sacred songs and published religious pamphlets. The printers' shop, carding machine, gristmill, wagon maker, and blacksmith shop are all shown on this 1835 drawing. The community was named for Watervliet, New York, the Shakers' first permanent settlement in America. (Warren County Historical Society.)

Garden seeds were stored in this cabinet made at Watervliet. Shakers in the West were selling a wide variety of garden seeds to the public by the 1820s. Watervliet Shakers often sold produce, herbs, and seeds at nearby Dayton's public markets. Brooms and woodenware were also sold widely to the public. (Golden Lamb Inn.)

This miller's house, shown on the drawing on page 57, is one of two surviving Watervliet buildings. The house was moved from the original village site to the grounds of the Kettering-Moraine Museum, Kettering, in 1983, and restored. A post-and-beam tannery barn was also salvaged from the village, dismantled, and stored in pieces for years before being reassembled by Amish workers in 1996 on the museum grounds. (Author's collection.)

Children dig in the dirt surrounding the new Mount St. John School in 1916. A Watervliet barn and house are seen in the background. Watervliet straddled the Montgomery-Greene County lines, with most of the land in Montgomery. The school was built on the Greene County side. The State of Ohio built the Dayton State Hospital farm on the Montgomery County side. (Warren County Historical Society.)

An abandoned frame Watervliet house, surrounded by debris, shows signs of neglect in this 1916 photograph. A barn is visible through the porch posts on the left. When Watervliet disbanded in 1910, its remaining 11 members moved to Union Village. (Warren County Historical Society.)

A solitary figure peers out of the third floor window of the impressive East House of the South Union, Kentucky, Shaker village in this *c.* 1885 photograph. The building bears an 1847 date, about the same time that Union Village's grand new Center House was also completed. South Union grew out of a group of religious dissenters who, like many of the Union Village Shakers, had participated in the Kentucky Revival in 1800. (Shaker Museum at South Union.)

A group of the world's people held a medical convention at South Union in 1911. A few Shakers are to the far left of the photograph. The group is posed in the west yard of the Center House with the meetinghouse in the background. Located in Logan County near the Kentucky-Tennessee border, South Union experienced considerable hardships during the Civil War but endured to become the West's longest-lived Shaker community at the time of its closing in 1922. (Shaker Museum at South Union.)

the citizens there would give them no shelter, but one man had promised to let them sleep in his hay mow, but before they reached the Town, he had locked it up, and would not let them in it: notwithstanding they were strong Secessionists & pretended to be their friends.

Nov 18th — John C Breckenridge with his Brigade passed thro' our village on the state road going to Russellville. He had five regiments, one of Cavalry and four of Infantry. They went to Russellville to guard and protect the Legislature, who had assembled there to form a provisional government for Ky.

They professed to be going on to Green River, they remained in Russelville for some days; We counted one hundred and ten wagons with their tents and provisions. The Artillery company had five cannon. They had little secesh flags and rags flying for ever company, some did not appear more than six or eight inches square flapping at the horses ears. There were some ten or fifteen negroes armed and equipped with deadly weapons marching with the Infantry, and others riding as waiters for their masters.

South Union's proximity to Russellville and Bowling Green, Kentucky, kept its Shakers embroiled in conflict during the Civil War. Kentucky declared its neutrality at the start of the war, but most citizens had firm convictions about the issues at stake. A committee met in Russellville in November 1861 to form a provisional Kentucky Confederate government. Bowling Green was soon named the state Confederate capital. Union and Confederate troops demanded food, water, horses, and supplies as they swept through South Union. Eldress Nancy E. Moore recorded the drama in her diary. Excerpts here from September 1861 tell of Gen. Simon B. Buckner's troops seizing Bowling Green and taking control of the railroads. "Now we know by experience what it is to be shut up in bondage," Moore wrote. In addition to the immediate hardships, the Shakers experienced the lingering economic effects of the war. Union Village responded with material aid and merchandise for the Kentucky Shakers to sell. (Dayton Metro Library.)

Sister Betsy Spaulding works at a loom in the Center Family dwelling at Pleasant Hill, Kentucky, in the 1890s. Spaulding came to Pleasant Hill in 1836 at age 11 and remained there until her death in 1905, serving as a children's caretaker, teacher, deaconess, and eldress at various times. Pleasant Hill began in 1806 and was supervised and assisted by Union Village elders for decades. (Shaker Village of Pleasant Hill, Harrodsburg, Kentucky.)

In this c. 1880 partial stereoscopic view, a group of Pleasant Hill Shakers gather at the West Family dwelling, built in 1822. Like Union Village, Pleasant Hill became known for its herbal medicines, garden seeds, and livestock. Beautiful textiles, brooms, woodenware, and tinware were also sold to the public. Pleasant Hill closed in 1910. In the 1960s, history lovers from the world reopened the restored village as a living museum, the largest Shaker historic site in the West. (Shaker Village of Pleasant Hill, Harrodsburg, Kentucky.)

This indenture made & entered into _____
this 13th day of July 1840 between Wm Coley
of Cty of Lexamind of State of Kentucky of the
One part & S.R Runyon of County of Mercer and
state aforesaid of the other part witnesseth that
said Coley doth this day put into the possession of
said Runyon three of his children buz Martha
Coley Mary Coley & Charles Coley which children
said William Coley doth hereby bind and obligate
himself not to disturb molest nor in any way
either directly or indirectly remove from the
possession of said Runyon untill they shall have
arrived to the years of maturity &c.

And Runyon on his part doth hereby bind
and obligate himself to grant or cause to be
granted unto said children the common priviled
-ges of the society of Shakers at Pleasant Hill
Mercer Cy. Kentucky Viz. of schooling clothing
shelter occupation religious instruction &c &c
provided withal that said children or either
of them does not leave said Runyon or Society
untill they are free as witness our hand this
day &c. &c.
Joseph H, Marshall

                                        his
                              William X Coley (S.S.)
                                        mark
                                        his
                              S.R Runyon X (S.S.)
                                        mark

Parents who found themselves in unfortunate circumstances sometimes entrusted their children to the Shakers. In this 1840 Pleasant Hill indenture document, William Coley agrees to allow the Shakers to raise and educate his son, Charles, and daughters, Martha and Nancy, until they reach the age of maturity. In return, the Shakers pledge to provide schooling, clothing, shelter, an occupation, and religious instruction to the children. Although the agreement was referred to as an indenture, it was not the type of indenture where people were sold into servitude for a specific number of years. The Shakers did hope, however, that the children would decide to join the faith when they reached adulthood. (Warren County Historical Society.)

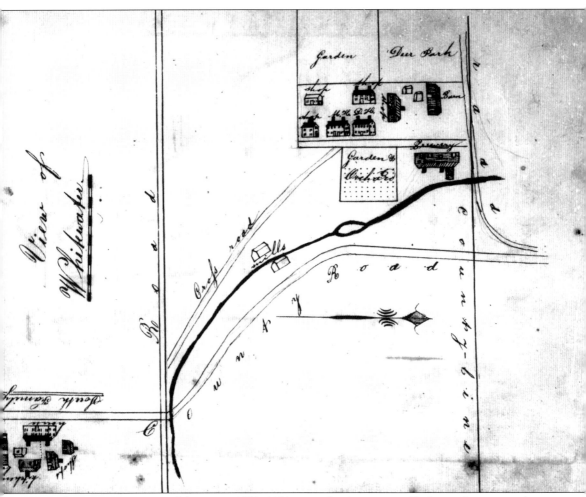

White Water, organized between 1822–1824, was the last major Shaker village started in Ohio. Like Watervliet, White Water was geographically close to Union Village. White Water eventually occupied 1,400 acres straddling the Hamilton and Butler County lines. This 1835 drawing shows the meetinghouse, family dwelling, numerous shops and barns, gardens and orchard, and a deer park as part of the North Family. The South Family included a dwelling, large kitchen, barn, shops, and other structures. The village grew to include another family, with the lifetime population of White Water estimated at 490. Agriculture, silk production, and broom manufacturing were important industries in the community. The White Water site, much of which is now owned by the Hamilton County Park District, holds the most original Shaker structures in the state. Friends of White Water Shaker Village are working to conserve and preserve the site. (Warren County Historical Society.)

Elder Stephen Ball kept this order book for the South Family at White Water in 1888. The book contains rules of conduct issued by the United Society of Believers' central ministry (now renamed Mount Lebanon) in 1887. Shaker leaders issued two other books of conduct, called *Millennial Laws*, in 1821 and 1845. (Dayton Metro Library.)

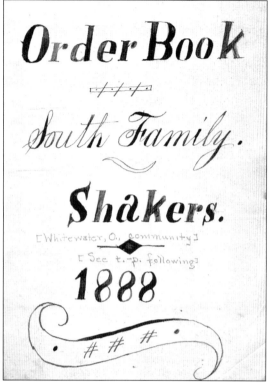

Union Village brothers traveled to White Water in 1827 to help build this brick meetinghouse. Union Village supported White Water spiritually and materially over the years as the smaller community struggled to grow. This structure is believed to be the only brick meetinghouse ever erected in a Shaker village. (Warren County Historical Society.)

Stephen W. Ball

Stephen. Ball

HIS. BOOK

in union with his brethren

"This is my 80th birthday. I am in the enjoyment of good health," wrote Stephen Ball in this notebook on June 24, 1895. Ball, who had previously lived at Watervliet, was an elder at White Water's North Family at the time. The notebook holds songs, poems, and meditations. (Dayton Metro Library.)

ior, of heaven above;

This little Anthem was coppied from a little gold plate Oct 6 1846 given by Mother. Ann,

Ball introduces the song reprinted on page 71 with a flourish, noting, "This little anthem was copied from a little gold plate Oct. 6, 1846, given by Mother Ann [Lee]." Shakers believed that songs, poems, instructions, and even metaphysical gifts such as the gold plate, came to them through divine revelation from Lee, Jesus, saints, and friends who were already in Heaven. (Dayton Metro Library.)

"Shout, Shout" is an example of a gift song, one that was given by a divine spirit to a Shaker on earth. Numerous gift drawings, such as the familiar Tree of Life, also came to members through revelations. During an especially intense time of spiritualism in the 1830s and 1840s, Shakers received hundreds of gift songs and drawings. (Dayton Metro Library.)

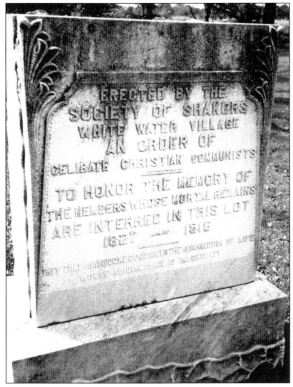

Shakers identify themselves as celibate Christian communists on this group tombstone at the White Water cemetery. Separate markers identify the graves of many Watervliet Shakers there. The cemetery, maintained by Crosby Township trustees, is open to the public. (Author's collection.)

Ralph Russell, shown here with wife, Laura, founded the North Union Shaker community near Cleveland between 1820 and 1824 after visiting Union Village members. But after a few years, the Russells left North Union to rejoin the world. The small community they started continued on until 1889, producing textiles, silk, brooms, and garden produce. Approximately 400 people practiced the Shaker faith there during the village's existence. (Elizabeth Nord Library, Shaker Historical Society Museum.)

This c. 1912 postcard shows North Union's transformation into the Cleveland suburb of Shaker Heights. Although no original North Union buildings remain, a number of Shaker artifacts, photographs, and research materials are available at the Shaker Historical Society Museum in Shaker Heights. (Author's collection.)

No matter what part of the country Shakers lived in, they stayed in touch through the written word. Shakers were great writers, producing thousands of letters, journal pages, songs, poems, magazines, and newspapers like the *Shaker*, published by the Watervliet, New York, community. This October 1871 issue lists contributing editors from each Shaker community. Charles Clapp represented Union Village. (Otterbein-Lebanon Archives.)

THE SHAKER.

▲

MONTHLY JOURNAL,

DEVOTED TO THE EXPOSITION OF RELIGION, ACCORDING TO SHAKER THEOLOGY.

FIFTY CENTS, PER ANNUM, IN ADVANCE.

G. A. LOMAS, Resident Editor, Shakers, Albany Co., N. Y.

MEMBERS OF SOCIETY

Appointed to answer Correspondents, among whom are the Board of Editors.

Elder F. W. Evans, Mt. Lebanon, Columbia Co., N. Y.
" Issachar Bates, Shakers, N. Y.
" Calvin G. Reed, Mt. Morris, Livingston Co., N. Y.
" Simon Mabee, West Pittsfield, Mass.
" Stoughton Kellogg, Thompsonville, Conn., Shakers.
" Albert Battles, Tyringham, Berkshire Co., Mass.
" Wm. Leonard, Ayer, Mass., Shakers.
" John Whiteley, Shirley Village, Middlesex Co., Mass.
" Nehemiah Trull, Shaker Village, Merrimack Co., N. H.
" Henry Cummings, Enfield, Grafton Co., N. H.
" John B. Vance, Alfred, Shakers, York Co., Me.
" Alonzo Gilman, West Gloucester, Cumberland Co., Me., Shakers.
" Chas. Clapp, Union Village, Warren Co., O., Shakers.
" Ezra Sherman, Preston, Hamilton Co., Ohio, Shakers.
" Stephen Ball, Dayton, Shakers, Ohio.
" Jacob Kulp, Pleasant Hill, Mercer Co., Ky.
" J. R. Eades, South Union, Logan Co., Ky.
" J. S. Prescott, Cleveland, Ohio, Shakers.

This dwelling in White Oak, Georgia, housed a small group of Union Village Shakers who began two Georgia colonies between 1898 and 1901. No expense was spared to make the White Oak dwelling attractive to potential converts. Yellow pine, Georgia oak, walnut, and marble were used in the construction. But the converts did not come, and by 1902, the Georgia properties were for sale. (Otterbein-Lebanon Archives.)

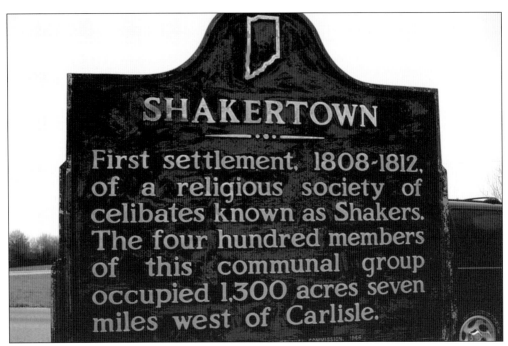

SHAKERTOWN

First settlement, 1808-1812, of a religious society of celibates known as Shakers. The four hundred members of this communal group occupied 1,300 acres seven miles west of Carlisle.

West Union, Indiana, was the most troubled western village. Between 1808 and 1827, when the colony was permanently abandoned, Shakers there suffered ramifications of the War of 1812 and devastating bouts of malaria. Elder John Dunlavy died there of fever in 1812, and Shakers fleeing the war unwittingly brought the deadly malaria back to Union Village. A state historical marker identifies the site near Vincennes on the Wabash River. (Michael Anderson.)

THE SHAKER

Gospel Treasures.

Should we take the bright wings of the morn
   And soar over mountain and sea,
From isles that old ocean adorn,
   To lands where the bright flowers be;
Should the mountains unbosom their gold,
   And ocean her jewels restore,
Should earth all her treasures unfold,
   Our spirits would still thirst for more.

There are far reaching depths in the soul,
   No phantoms of pleasure can fill;
There are wild waves of passions that roll,
   No power but of Heaven can still :
There's a heart sad and lonely within,
   A hunger for good from above;
There's a deep seated sorrow for sin,
   And thirst for pure Heavenly love.

There's a happiness purity brings,
   Contentment the gospel bestows;
There's a hope in the trusting heart springs,
   Triumphant o'er earth and its woes :
There's a treasure of bliss far away,
   Reserved for the righteous in store;
And the bright morn is dawning to-day
   That never knows night any more.

There are pleasures that never grow old,
   And hopes that will never decay;
There's a wealth that is richer than gold,
   To all who the gospel obey.
Rejoice, then, ye faithful and true,
   Your day of salvation has come;
The bright crown of glory in view,
   Invites to your Heavenly home.
               E. T. LEGGETT.
UNION VILLAGE, Ohio, Aug. 1871.

Ezra T. Leggitt's "Gospel Treasures," printed in the October 1871 issue of the *Shaker*, expresses a common theme in Shaker literature. A respected member of Union Village, Leggitt shared his faith through his poems and essays. Leggitt also represented the western Shaker communities during an 1862 meeting with Pres. Abraham Lincoln and Secretary of War Edwin Stanton, where Shakers sought exemption from the draft. (Otterbein-Lebanon Archives.)

Five

THE HEART
OF THE VILLAGE

Pupils pose in front of the Union Village School in this c. 1890s photograph. Shakers opened their first school for members' children in 1808, at a time when only well-to-do neighbors could afford to send their children to one of the few subscription schools in the county. Literacy for each Shaker was a community goal. Within a few decades, Shaker schools became known for excellence in the academic fundamentals. By the 1860s, neighborhood children also attended the Shaker schools while Union Village teachers took the state teaching exam in Lebanon beside the world's educators. (Warren County Historical Society.)

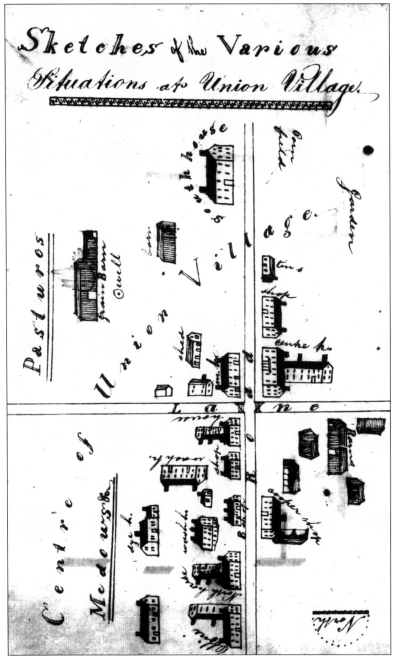

Brother George Kendall's 1835 drawing of the village's center shows the meetinghouse on the east side of the road, just south of where the lane intersects. The meetinghouse remained in that location until 1965. It was truly the heart of the community. Two eldresses and two elders, who led the Shakers, lived on the second floor of the meetinghouse. The most devout members lived in the First (or Center) Family that is shown directly across the road from the meetinghouse in 1835. Spiritual and temporal leadership radiated out of the village's center. Early converts Malcolm Worley, Richard McNemar, Calvin Morrell, Samuel Rollins, and David Johnson all donated their land to form the core of Union Village. (Warren County Historical Society.)

The old and the new coexist in this *c.* 1950s aerial photograph of the Otterbein Home. State Route 741 runs through the middle of the village. The highway opened as a county road in 1807, insuring that the Shakers would never be totally cloistered from the world. The public literally traveled through their midst daily, passing the four major buildings that formed the heart of Union Village. The trustees' office, identified by its twin turrets and center tower, is in the foreground on the west side of State Route 741. Across the highway is the old meetinghouse. Located across the yard, just north of the meetinghouse is the Old Center House, completed by the Shakers in 1819. Across the road is the New Center House (the large brick T-shaped dwelling), completed in 1846. To the north of the New Center House is Phillippi Hall, which Otterbein completed in 1935. Phillippi Hall was built for residences, business offices, a chapel, dining room, and kitchen. (Otterbein-Lebanon Archives.)

Isaac Liddell gave his daughter, Susanna Cole Liddell, to the Shakers in 1835 when she was 11 years old. She became a prominent member who wrote extensively about her spiritual experiences and about the community's history. Susanna's nephew, Granville Hixson, who worked for the United Brethren Church, was instrumental in starting discussions that led to the United Society selling the village's property to the United Brethren Church. Susanna died in 1914. (Otterbein-Lebanon Archives.)

Hundreds of students studied reading, writing, arithmetic, elocution, grammar, and geography in Union Village's schoolhouse over the years. Boys and girls attended school during separate months when the school opened in 1808. Separate schedules accommodated the Shakers' separation of the sexes and also allowed the boys to help with the autumn harvest. (Otterbein-Lebanon Archives.)

The stack of books near Oliver Hampton's arm hints at his roles as elder, schoolteacher, and writer during his 79 years at Union Village. Oliver's parents, Charles D. and Julia Carey Hampton, brought their family of six to Union Village in 1822. Oliver, who admired his parents deeply, followed in their footsteps. He formerly joined the faith at age 12 and eventually taught at the village school as his mother had and served as an elder. Oliver remembered the early members of the community and was an enthusiastic advocate for Shakerism. He taught at the village school for close to 40 years and served on the Warren County Board of Education. He wrote numerous poems, essays, and meditations for Shaker publications and defended his faith in secular newspapers as well. He also wrote an important history of Union Village in the last few years of his life. His older sister, Emily, was also a lifelong member of the community who worked as a seamstress and served as an eldress. (Warren County Historical Society.)

The main road into the village (later to be State Route 741) is still unpaved in this *c.* 1900 photograph. The office, water tower, and some barns are visible in the distance to the left of the road. (Otterbein-Lebanon Archives.)

This *c.* 1910 postcard of the same view features some cattle grazing and a car seemingly en route to the village. As more people purchased cars in the early 1900s, Union Village became a destination for afternoon drives. Visitors might walk through the village's beautiful grounds, stopping to buy some of the sisters' fancywork or fruit preserves. (Otterbein-Lebanon Archives.)

Multiple doors and steps into the meetinghouse point out the Shaker custom of men and women entering by separate doors. They also sat separately at worship. Visitors could attend Sabbath services. They too entered by a separate door and sat in a visitors' section inside. (Warren County Historical Society.)

The Old Center House, completed in 1819, became a residence for around 40 elderly Otterbein residents after the United Brethren Church bought the village. Otterbein people called the building Old Bethany. (Otterbein-Lebanon Archives.)

A group of Otterbein women pose in front of the meetinghouse in this c. 1930s photograph. The Bibles and hymnals suggest they were either going to or returning from worship. (Otterbein-Lebanon Archives.)

This postcard from the early 20th century shows the relationship between the meetinghouse to the left and the trustee' office to the right. About 20 Shakers still lived in Union Village when Otterbein took over. Some of them left for other homes, while those who remained lived in the trustees' office, which had been grandly renovated in the 1890s. (Otterbein-Lebanon Archives.)

The meetinghouse serves as a quiet backdrop for Otterbein young people enjoying a snowy afternoon in the 1930s. Otterbein officials updated the meetinghouse several times over four decades. At one point, awnings shaded the bottom windows. Eventually a covered porch was added to the front. (Otterbein-Lebanon Archives.)

The campus between the trustees' office (left) and meetinghouse is filled with children playing and adults walking to various destinations in this c. 1930s view. The spacious lawns of the community provided a natural playground over the years for both Shaker and Otterbein children. (Otterbein-Lebanon Archives.)

When the meetinghouse was deemed unusable, Otterbein officials offered it to Warren County firefighters for a fire training exercise on March 6, 1965. Ruth and Warren McMichael snapped the photographs on this page and page 85 as the exercise progressed. Here a small crowd gathers as firefighters prepare to begin. (Lebanon-Otterbein Archives)

Even after the fire has gutted the meetinghouse, walnut rafters and brick chimneys still stand as proof of Shaker workmanship. Inside are the remains of two fireplaces: one over five feet wide and one six and a half feet wide. (Otterbein-Lebanon Archives.)

Smoke and flames fill the air as the meetinghouse burns. During Union Village's day, the second floor held two bedrooms: one for the top two elders and one for the top two eldresses. The men and women ascended to their rooms via double staircases. Latticework in the walls of the enclosed stairways allowed the leaders to monitor the Shakers worshipping below. (Otterbein-Lebanon Archives.)

At the end of the day, crumbled bricks and supports are all that remains of the meetinghouse. In the background, the 1846 Center House, now called New Bethany, still stands. (Otterbein-Lebanon Archives.)

Around 65 Otterbein boys lived in New Bethany when this photograph was taken around 1933. When it was completed in 1846, the building became home to 112 Shakers of Union Village's First Family. The building featured a large communal dining room and a meeting room that held 200. (Otterbein-Lebanon Archives.)

The mulberry trees on the lawn between New Bethany and the trustees' office had originally been planted by the Shakers to assist in their silk industry. Sisters raised silkworms in the mulberry trees, spun their silk, and used the fabric in trims for their own clothing and in more elaborate textiles that were sold to the world. (Otterbein-Lebanon Archives.)

Ellen Ross was two years old when she and her three siblings came to live at Union Village in 1838. Her parents, Mary and John, were English immigrants; John had been born in Manchester, the hometown of Shaker founder Ann Lee. The Shakers at Union Village educated Ellen as well as her sister, Harriett, and brothers, Andrew and John. Young Andrew became a helper in the shoemakers' shop. Ellen learned a variety of domestic skills as she continued to study the Shaker faith. By 1880, she was Union Village's second eldress. She assisted the lead, or first, eldress, in instructing new women members and counseling other sisters. Along with the first eldress and first and second elders, she lived in the meetinghouse in the village's center where the leaders were accessible and visible to the entire community. In this c. 1900 photograph, Ellen wears her Sabbath dress and cape, and the ever-present white linen cap worn by Shaker women well into the 20th century. (Warren County Historical Society.)

Shown here about 1916, the Old Center House, or Old Bethany, was remodeled by Otterbein trustees in 1918 when it was 100 years old. It became known as the Old People's Home, housing about 30–40 residents at a time. (Otterbein-Lebanon Archives.)

Old Bethany shows its age in this 1948 photograph by Warren County resident Jim Waters. As the practicality of remodeling the building for residents' use diminished and new construction continued at Otterbein, Old Bethany was eventually abandoned as a residence. Efforts to find an outside organization to move Old Bethany to another site for restoration failed. (Otterbein-Lebanon Archives.)

On October 9, 1965, Old Bethany met the same fate that the meetinghouse had just five months earlier. The building's shell remained, even after the Lebanon Fire Department let a training fire burn out of control for three hours. A bulldozer was brought in to flatten the remaining walls. (Otterbein-Lebanon Archives.)

The North Family dwelling, shown here in 1916, was built in 1823. The home sheltered hundreds of Shakers over the years, before it became a residence for Otterbein seniors. Otterbein added the front porch during an early renovation. (Otterbein-Lebanon Archives.)

This elders' shop, shown around 1933, was one of the first brick structures, built by the Shakers in 1811 after they started making their own bricks. In addition to spiritually leading members, each elder and eldress had another vocation to keep them grounded and humble. (Otterbein-Lebanon Archives.)

This later view of the elders' shop shows a two-story addition that came from a Shaker building in the South Family Lot. The Shakers later used the building as a carpenter's shop and as their post office. Otterbein used the shop, remodeled and renamed Rose Cottage, as a girls' dormitory for several years. (Otterbein-Lebanon Archives.)

In the early 1970s, a group of concerned Shaker enthusiasts, Otterbein administrators, and members of the Warren County Historical Society, gathered together to preserve Rose Cottage. Plans were discussed to try to find outside funding to restore the building on site or move it to another location where the public would have more access to it. (Otterbein-Lebanon Archives.)

COMMITTEE FOR THE RESTORATION OF THE SHAKER'S UNION VILLAGE

You are invited to be a part of a "Working Committee" to insure the preservation of this, the earliest Shaker Brick Structure in Ohio, as well as an important part of the life and history of our state.

Employees of the Armco Steel plant in Middletown paint and repair Rose Cottage in April 1970. Armco Steel had shown an interest in Union Village's history since purchasing part of the property from Otterbein to use as an employee park. Efforts to persuade the Ohio Historical Society to restore and maintain Rose Cottage ultimately failed, and the building was razed. (Otterbein-Lebanon Archives.)

Shakers rest near the front door of the trustees' office in this photograph from the late 1880s. The frame structure was built in 1810 as a residence for Shakers, but when the larger Center House was completed, trustees moved into the older building. Trustees conducted the village's business affairs from the trustees' office and entertained visitors from the world there. (Warren County Historical Society.)

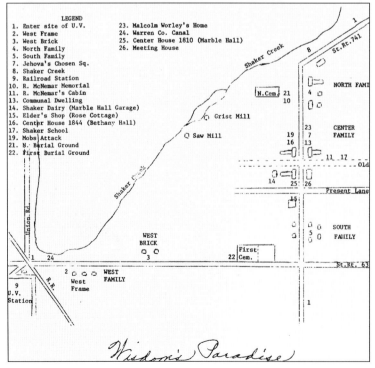

LEGEND

1. Enter site of U.V.
2. West Frame
3. West Brick
4. North Family
5. South Family
7. Jehova's Chosen Sq.
8. Shaker Creek
9. Railroad Station
10. R. McNemar Memorial
11. R. McNemar's Cabin
13. Communal Dwelling
14. Shaker Dairy (Marble Hall Garage)
15. Elder's Shop (Rose Cottage)
16. Center House 1844 (Bethany Hall)
17. Shaker School
19. Mobs Attack
21. N. Burial Ground
22. First Burial Ground
23. Malcolm Worley's Home
24. Warren Co. Canal
25. Center House 1810 (Marble Hall)
26. Meeting House

Irene Lane's map of Union Village shows the relationship of the trustees' office, meetinghouse, and the Old and New Center Houses to the rest of the community. Jehovah's Chosen Square, which probably was located a bit farther east, was where the Shakers' held special outdoor worship services during a period of intense spiritualism in the 1830s and 1840s. (Warren County Historical Society.)

With the population down to about 60, Elder Joseph Slingerland decided in 1891 to remodel the trustees' office in an attempt to attract new members. The Shakers were unprepared for the magnitude of the renovation. Turrets, a tower, porches, elaborate trim, and a new roofline all but obliterated the building's original facade. Inside the changes were even more striking. In place of simple, unadorned spaces, the Shakers now had floors, vanities, and tabletops of marble. The use of marble was so extensive that, after Otterbein took over, the building was known as Marble Hall. The foyer boasted a beautiful stairway crafted of solid butternut wood. Dark stained doors and woodwork complimented the original traditional Shaker built-ins. Updated bathrooms and kitchen provided luxurious accommodations that rivaled any of the grand Federal and Victorian homes in the county seat of Lebanon. The new trustees' office was beautiful, but definitely not Shaker. The renovation, plus some questionable business dealings by Slingerland, indebted the village for years but did not attract a significant number of new members. (Otterbein-Lebanon Archives.)

Rich paneled doors and woodwork in Marble Hall were added during the 1890s renovation. (Otterbein-Lebanon Archives.)

Butternut was used in the Marble Hall staircases. At the time of remodeling, Slingerland ordered interior furnishings that were more in keeping with contemporary style. Draperies, carpets, and wallpaper began to be used in the building. (Otterbein-Lebanon Archives.)

The trustees' office's turrets and central tower became landmarks for travelers approaching Union Village from all directions. Some of the changes, such as the side porches, provided a practical touch that made the building more pleasant for its inhabitants. (Otterbein-Lebanon Archives.)

An important part of the trustees' office renovation was the construction of the engine/boiler house at the rear of the dwelling in 1893. The boiler house aided in heating the trustees' office and provided hot water for residents. (Otterbein-Lebanon Archives.)

This c. 1900 photograph gives a sense of the size of the trustees' office. The woman in the foreground does not appear to be wearing a cap and is probably not a Shaker. To the far left, three sisters are dwarfed by the tree. (Warren County Historical Society.)

Ice-covered trees and a snowy carpet make the trustees' office resemble a fairy tale castle in this *c*. 1900 photograph. By then, the building resembled more of a late Victorian mansion on a Christmas card rather than a Shaker building. (Otterbein-Lebanon Archives.)

THE FIRST SETTLEMENT OF THE
SYMMES PURCHASE LANDS
IN WARREN COUNTY
WAS LOCATED A SHORT DISTANCE
SOUTH-WEST OF HERE
BY WILLIAM BEEDLE IN 1795

DEDICATED BY
WARREN COUNTY HISTORICAL SOCIETY
SEPTEMBER 23-1945

This marker, about one mile south of the trustees' office, honors William Beedle, founder of Beedle's Station, the first permanent settlement in Warren County around 1795. Several families with the surname of Bedle or Beedle were among the early Shaker converts at Union Village who donated their property to the sect. (Author's collection.)

This Union Village cupboard on display at the Warren County Historical Society illustrates regional differences in furnishings. Corner cupboards are found only at Union Village and Pleasant Hill. Shaker expert Charles R. Muller believes the cupboards show a German influence. Records show that many Union Village residents were of German ancestry. (Author's collection.)

Six

UNION VILLAGE AND THE WORLD

Missionaries from Union Village began a complex relationship with Shawnee warrior Tecumseh and his brother the Prophet in 1807 that had far-reaching repercussions for the village. The Prophet had initiated a spiritual revival among a small band of Shawnee that he and Tecumseh gathered at Greenville. The Shakers and Shawnees exchanged visits throughout the summer, discussing their respective beliefs and observing each other's worship. The Shakers hoped to convert the Shawnees; the Shawnees hoped to gain the trust of white secular leaders. Both sides were ultimately disappointed, but the visits did bear some fruit. The Shawnees gained some much-needed supplies and trading contacts, and the Shakers gained an appreciation for the Shawnee religion. Unfortunately the Shakers' opponents used the relationship as a reason to attack the Shakers in print, in court, and in several mob actions for almost 10 years. (Library of Congress.)

Warren County farmer and statesman Jeremiah Morrow was an early admirer of the Shaker livestock industry. In 1812, while serving as Ohio's first congressman, Morrow noticed the Shakers' success with the merino sheep that they were importing from Spain. Morrow introduced the breed to his township, and the wool industry in Warren County took off in earnest. (Warren County Historical Society.)

Hamilton businessman and historian James McBride came to scoff at the Shakers one Sabbath in 1811. In one of the most detailed outsider descriptions of Union Village at that time, McBride conceded that the Shakers were industrious, healthy, and prosperous. He was still critical, however, of their religious practices, particularly the separation of children and parents. (Butler County Historical Society.)

JAMES McBRIDE.

Icabod Corwin, Lebanon's first settler, was one of the influential county residents who advocated tolerance of the Shakers' religious rights. Corwin was closely connected with Francis Dunlavy, the teacher and judge whose brother John became a prominent Shaker elder. Corwin is also remembered for building the Black Horse Tavern, Lebanon's first business and site for early sessions of county court. (Warren County Historical Society.)

Corwin owned the Green Tree Tavern, just northwest of Union Village, while he was a conductor on the Underground Railroad. Escaped slaves traveled through the heart of Union Village from the Green Tree Tavern to a station in the Warren County hamlet of Red Lion. The situation proved difficult for the Shakers, who practiced racial equality but were forbidden from political action. (Dr. C. Nelson Melampy.)

Pres. William Henry Harrison's association with the Shakers dates back to 1811 when he was governor of the Indiana Territory. The Shakers were struggling to establish a community on the banks of the Wabash River in what is now Knox County, Indiana. The settlement of Busro, later called West Union, was frequented by groups of Native Americans whom the Shakers were eager to befriend. Harrison closely monitored the Shakers' dealings with the Native Americans and protected the Shakers from settlers who did not like their lifestyle or their friends. While Harrison defended the Shakers' civil and religious freedoms, he later wrote that the Shakers naively allowed themselves to be used by the Native Americans. Harrison defeated their old friend the Prophet at Tippecanoe, Indiana, in 1811 and led troops in the Canadian battle of 1813 where Tecumseh was killed. Harrison later visited Union Village multiple times before his election as president and untimely, his death in 1841. The Shakers, being apolitical, did not take a position on Harrison's candidacy. (Library of Congress.)

Thomas Corwin, a longtime friend of the Shakers' and a nationally known statesman, successfully defended Union Village in an Ohio Supreme Court case of the 1840s that could have literally torn the community apart. The case began in 1844 after the death of Malcolm Worley, the first western convert. Worley was venerated by most Shakers, but he and two other early converts clashed with an elder from the East in the 1830s, and their roles in the village were diminished. Worley's three children, who were also prominent Shakers, apparently could not forget the insult he had suffered. After Worley's death, the children left Union Village and sued to recover the land that he and his wife had given to the United Society in 1808. The property was in the heart of the village. Its loss would have left a physical and emotional hole in Union Village. The case dragged on for four years with Corwin—then a U.S. senator—defending the Shakers in the Supreme Court. Corwin was a relative of Icabod Corwin, shown on page 101. (Warren County Historical Society.)

An older, distinguished Thomas Corwin is shown in the portrait hanging in the study of his Lebanon home. When in town, Corwin often received clients in his book-lined study. The Shakers may have consulted with him there about the Worley case, or he may have met with them in the trustees' office at Union Village. (Warren County Historical Society.)

Corwin's large home on Main Street in Lebanon was a landmark even in his day. The Shakers would have passed it every time they came into town. Corwin was one of the great orators of his day, comparable to Henry Clay, another Union Village visitor. Corwin served Ohio as a congressman, governor, and senator. He served the nation as secretary of the treasury and as ambassador to Mexico. (Otterbein-Lebanon Archives.)

Electa Jacobs and her husband, Enoch, were among approximately 200 Millerites who joined Union Village and White Water in 1846, after their founder William Miller incorrectly predicted the date that Jesus Christ would return to earth. The Jacobses left Union Village in 1847 but remained interested in spiritualism. They and three of their children are buried in Warren County's Miami Cemetery. (Warren County Historical Society.)

Enoch published the *Day-Star* newspaper in 1846 and 1847 while living at Union Village. He also spoke frequently at religious meetings and the Shakers hoped, in vain, that he would become a missionary for the sect. Jacobs had been prominent in the Millerite movement in Ohio before joining the Shakers and had published a millennial newspaper, the *Midnight Cry*, in Cincinnati. (Library of Congress.)

Richard Realf, the former secretary of state in abolitionist John Brown's provisional government, sought sanctuary at Union Village in 1860. He had just testified before a special Senate committee in Washington that he had broken off with Brown before the Harper's Ferry raid was planned. Realf stayed with the Shakers for several months, preaching against intemperance at public meetings, then left to join Union troops. (Library of Congress.)

Dixon's Opera House in Hamilton was the scene of the Shakers' largest public meeting held outside of Union Village. Still seeking converts in 1874, Shakers from Union Village and Watervliet joined together to address a crowd of almost 1,000 people who paid 25¢ or 50¢ to hear about Shaker beliefs on celibacy, women's rights, pacifism, and communal living. (Author's collection.)

As private companies competed with Shaker products, the Shakers began using more secular advertising to promote their industries. This broadside for Union Village's sarsaparilla stresses the purity of the product, provides testimonials, and warns consumers against imitators. A directive to look for TrusteePeter Boyd's signature on the bottle emphasizes the Shaker brand. The advertisement also includes directions for taking the medicine. Patients were to eat a light, nutritious diet and abstain from alcohol and fermented drinks. Shakers had also been leaders in providing planting directions on small packets of seeds for home gardeners, a marketing innovation created at Union Village. In the early days of the seed industry, Shakers stressed that their seeds were grown in their communities. But as this advertisement demonstrates, they were not averse to importing materials when necessary. The increased demand for sarsaparilla led them to import sarsaparilla roots from South America. What made the sarsaparilla effective, they affirmed, was the Shaker preparation of it. (Dr. M. Stephen and Miriam R. Miller.)

Clarence and Nellie (Guthermuth) Melampy went to live with the Shakers after their marriage in 1906. Clarence followed his father's example in farming for the Shakers. His father, James H. Melampy, used to come to Union Village from the nearby village of Monroe with his sister and brothers as children to do chores for the Shakers. As a young man around 1880, James began working with the Shakers full time. They trained him as a herdsman. His brother Bill was trained as a horseman and took charge of the stallions on the farm. As Clarence worked with the Shakers, he supervised a group of hired hands that helped him farm. The 1900 Warren County directory lists these tenants living at Union Village: Edwin Cullen, P. Hackett, David Hackett, James Hackett, Robert Kennedy, Pat Melampy, who was James's brother, and Phillip Ryan, who was married to James's sister Margaret. (Dr. C. Nelson Melampy.)

Clarence and Nellie Melampy lived here in the North Family dwelling with the Shakers after their marriage. Their son Dr. C. Nelson Melampy credits the sisters with teaching his mother, a former schoolteacher, to be a good farm homemaker. This included cooking Shaker dishes, preserving food, and curing meat. The training served the family well during the Great Depression, when they were farming on their own. (Otterbein-Lebanon Archives.)

Clarence Melampy (left) and former hired hand John Neil reminisce about their younger days working with the Shakers. Tenant farmers like Melampy worked on shares, splitting their profits with the Shakers. Neil was one of the hands whom Melampy supervised on the Shaker farm. Clarence and Nellie left Union Village around 1913 and later bought their own farm in the Mason area. (Dr. C. Nelson Melampy.)

James H. Melampy farmed for the Gristmill Family of Shakers on the west side of the village. He lived in the Gristmill house, shown at left in 1919 after it stood unused for many years. After retiring from farming, James lived in the Green Tree Tavern house, shown on page 101, for some time. (Dr. C. Nelson Melampy.)

As the 20th century commenced and the Shakers were fading away, John P. MacLean, a Warren County journalist and history buff, began interviewing the remaining members of the community and researching the Shakers' past. MacLean published this important biography of Richard McNemar in 1905. MacLean interviewed more Ohio Shakers than any previous writer and, in 1907, published *Shakers of Ohio: Fugitive Papers Concerning the Shakers of Ohio, With Unpublished Manuscripts*. (Warren County Historical Society.)

A

SKETCH

OF THE

LIFE AND LABORS

OF

RICHARD MCNEMAR

BY

J. P. MACLEAN

Edition Limited to 250 Copies

Price 50 Cents

FRANKLIN, OHIO
Printed for the Author by
THE FRANKLIN CHRONICLE
1905

Seven

THE OTTERBEIN YEARS

The tradition of providing for children in need continued when the United Brethren Church purchased Union Village from the United Society of Believers in 1912 to form Otterbein Home. Some children were orphans; others were children of missionaries who were working aboard. This c. 1913 photograph shows two early groups of children. The group to the left shows, from left to right, Elizabeth, Everett, and Mary Owen of Wabash, Indiana. The other group includes, from left to right, Blanch, Mildred, and Goldie Clark of Springfield. In addition to caring for children, the Otterbein Home cared for the elderly and the infirm. (Otterbein-Lebanon Archives.)

OTTERBEIN HOME MANAGEMENT
EXECUTIVE COMMITTEE—Funk, Miller, Phillippi

Superintendent
J. R. King

Matron
Zella B. King

FARM COMMITTEE—Gerlaugh, McClure, Judy
HOUSE COMMITTEE— Mathews, Griffis, Davisson, Howard

Otterbein officials in 1916 included, from left to right, (first row, the Women's Advisory Committee) Mrs. G. M. Mathews, Dayton; Mrs. G. F. Griffis, Eaton; Mrs. J. A. Davisson, Dayton; and Mrs. A. T. Howard, Dayton; (second row, the Farm Committee) J. A. Gerlaugh of Dayton; J. R. McClure of Harrison; and Harry Judy of Germantown; (third row) Dr. John R. and Zella B. King, who served as the first superintendent and matron respectively; (fourth row) W. R. Funk, chairman; L. O. Miller, treasurer; and J. M. Phillippi, secretary. (Otterbein-Lebanon Archives.)

An Otterbein photographer snapped these girls on their way to the laundry around 1916. Like the Shakers, Otterbein Home officials believed children needed to be taught how to perform a variety of tasks and to be self-sufficient. (Otterbein-Lebanon Archives.)

The first six children arrived at Otterbein on May 1, 1913. They were, from left to right, Russell, Leona, and Carl Shimer from Carey and Robert, Byron, and Harold Dickensheets of Dayton. Both groups of children had lost their mothers. Superintendent John R. King used to collect new arrivals at the Red Lion interurban station, and take them to the village in a carriage drawn by a horse called Old Bubba. (Otterbein-Lebanon Archives.)

Eight governesses, or house parents, pose in this c. 1922 photograph. Children were separated by sex and age and cared for by a governess along with their peers. Last names only are given for these women seen here, from left to right, Pidgley, Smith, Rule, Esbenshade, Mattox, Botkin, Alger, and Cox. (Otterbein-Lebanon Archives.)

Sister Lucy Hunt was one of 10 women from the Canterbury, New Hampshire, Shaker community, who came to Union Village to care for the remaining members there, beginning in 1912. The Canterbury sisters and the Union Village Shakers lived in the trustees' office but participated in many aspects of Otterbein life. Hunt had the longest tenure of the Canterbury sisters, staying until the last Union Village residents left in 1920. (Warren County Historical Society.)

Residents of Old Bethany dined in style around 1915. Otterbein renovated the building to make it comfortable for its elderly inhabitants. Tablecloths and white napkins provided a homey touch. (Otterbein-Lebanon Archives.)

The Canterbury sisters blended into their new situation well. Union Village had long enjoyed a cordial family and business relationship with the older community that was founded in 1792. By 1912, Canterbury was one of the largest remaining communities in the East. The sisters shown here are all from Canterbury; the brothers are from Union Village. Seen here are, from left to right, (first row, seated) Trustee James Fennessey, Aida Elam, and Eldress Mary Ann Wilson; (second row, standing) Hope Vicery and George Baxter. While the men's clothes in 1916 appear similar to their worldly counterparts, the women maintain their traditional Shaker dress. The trustees' office where they lived is in the background. (Otterbein-Lebanon Archives.)

The Pilcher children of St. Elmo, Illinois, were living at Otterbein in 1915 when this picture was taken. Seen here are, from left to right, Harold, William, Leslie, Francis, and Elmer. Their sister, Rhoda, also lived at Otterbein but is not in the picture. The older children—whether relatives or not—were encouraged to look after the younger ones. (Otterbein-Lebanon Archives.)

A group of youngsters play London Bridge around 1913. The house parents at Otterbein aimed to provide fun, love, and spiritual nurturing in addition to food and shelter to their charges. (Otterbein-Lebanon Archives.)

Superintendent John R. King snapped this picture of two happy boys on the steps of New Bethany around 1916. Shaker Trustee James Fennessey's unhappy childhood in a Cincinnati orphanage motivated him to see that a benevolent organization that would kindly care for children took over the village. Fennessey also endowed a small scholarship to enable orphans to attend Otterbein College in Ohio. (Otterbein-Lebanon Archives.)

Laundry, meals, and baths for hundreds of children, senior citizens, and staff required an up-to-date water system. Fortunately Otterbein inherited Union Village's extensive water system, which it improved and expanded over the years. Here the water tower in the background and water hydrant in the foreground indicate some of the community's resources. (Otterbein-Lebanon Archives.)

Four of the Canterbury sisters pose with James Fennessey on the village grounds around 1915. Lucy Hunt is in the foreground. Hope Vickery is to the left, Aida Elam is seated behind Hunt, and Eldress Mary Ann Wilson stands behind Fennessey. (Otterbein-Lebanon Archives.)

W. T. Markee of Iowa (left) and an unidentified helper paint the trustees' office building in 1924. By this time, the trustees' office was needed for Otterbein people. The remaining Shakers and their Canterbury assistants had moved out in 1920. A few of the Union Village women moved to Canterbury to live; others went to various homes. (Otterbein-Lebanon Archives.)

The whole community—Otterbein and Shaker—turned out for the 1916 church picnic. Several sisters are recognizable by their white caps. The harp was presumably for the afternoon's entertainment. Behind the group is the trustees' office, later called Marble Hall. After the Shakers vacated the building in 1920, Otterbein continued to use the building as a residence. Women employees were living there by the early 1960s. The building was unused from 1964 to 1971, when Otterbein undertook a $30,000 renovation of the structure. Marble Hall now contains resident apartments, business offices, the archives office, Shaker Room and Attic Museum, Otterbein Room, and some storage facilities. (Otterbein-Lebanon Archives.)

Superintendent John R. King and his wife, Zella, relax in their living room around 1913. Picture rails have replaced Shaker peg rails, and the furnishings reflect upper-middle-class comfort of the period. The accommodations were particularly comfortable for the Kings, who returned to the United States in 1912 after 18 years of missionary work in Sierra Leone, West Africa. (Otterbein-Lebanon Archives.)

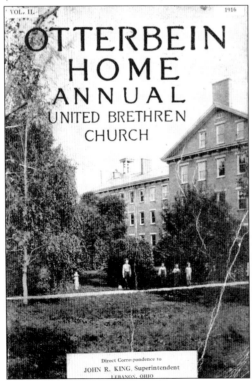

The *Otterbein Home Annual* was started as an educational and fund-raising publication in 1915. Articles in the early editions frequently discuss the Shakers and their heritage. Children pose near New Bethany for this 1916 cover. (Otterbein-Lebanon Archives.)

Eldress Mary Ann Wilson (front row, second from left) poses with her sisters in 1914 at Canterbury before leaving to supervise other Canterbury sisters at Union Village. Wilson served at Union Village from August 31, 1915, to June 20, 1920. The sisters donned their Sabbath best for the portrait. (Otterbein-Lebanon Archives.)

The Union Village sisters who moved to Canterbury in 1920 lived here in the East Family dwelling. Canterbury was one of the longest-lived Shaker communities, with its last member, Sister Ethel Hudson, dying in 1992. Canterbury is now open to the public as a historic site, although not all of the buildings are accessible. (Author's collection.)

James Fennessey smiles in the middle of an Otterbein entourage visiting Canterbury in 1918. Otterbein officials presented the Canterbury Shakers with an inscribed loving cup. The Shakers later sent Otterbein two Guernsey cattle named Canterbury Queen and Otterbein King. (Otterbein-Lebanon Archives.)

The infirmary at Canterbury is where the Union Village sisters would have gone for treatment in their final years. The refurbished building is open to visitors. A sampling of the medicinal herbs grown by the Shakers, including mint and bee balm, is planted along the front walk. (Author's collection.)

THE
OTTERBEIN
HOME

From Two States

From Three Parsonages

This certificate, when properly signed by the officials of the Otterbein Home, a corporation chartered under the laws of the state of Ohio, is evidence that

Mr. and Mrs. H. W. King.

of *Duluth Minne.*   is a friend of religious and philanthropic work, and

Has paid for One Acre of the Otterbein Home Farm

in the acreage plot distribution in the celebration of the tenth anniversary of the purchase of the Shaker estate of four thousand and five acres, near Lebanon. Ohio, on March fifth, nineteen hundred and thirteen.

President
Secretary
Treasurer

Otterbein issued commemorative certificates on the home's 10th anniversary to acknowledge donors who had paid for one acre of farmland. The certificate notes the 1913 official transfer of the property and includes a dramatic photograph of the trustees' office. (Otterbein-Lebanon Archives.)

Robert H. and Virginia Jones furnished the Shaker Dining Room at their Golden Lamb Inn in Lebanon with artifacts from Union Village and other Shaker communities. The Joneses were leaders in celebrating local Shaker heritage. Much of their collection is exhibited, along with pieces loaned by Otterbein, at the Warren County Historical Society in Lebanon. The Shaker Dining Room, along with other Shaker pieces, is still intact at the Golden Lamb Inn. (Author's collection.)

Brother Arnold Hadd and Sister Frances Carr of Sabbathday Lake, Maine, view some of the historic Union Village photographs during a 1982 visit to the Otterbein-Lebanon Retirement Community. This was Carr's second visit to the community; she first visited in 1974. (Otterbein-Lebanon Archives.)

Shakers from Sabbathday Lake visited the Otterbein-Lebanon Retirement Community in November 1974 to celebrate the sect's bicentennial. During the two-day visit, they toured Otterbein, the Warren County Museum, and the White Water settlement. Seen here are, from left to right, Brother Ted Johnson, Sister Mildred Barker, Hazel Spenser Phillips, and Carr. Phillips was the former director of the Warren County Historical Society who researched and wrote extensively about Union Village. (Otterbein-Lebanon Archives.)

A highway project on State Route 741 led to an archeological dig at the former North Family dwelling and pottery shop in the spring of 2005. Teams from the Ohio Department of Transportation and the Columbus firm of Hard Lines Design staked out the outlines of the original buildings and painstakingly uncovered thousands of brick segments, pottery pieces, and pottery making equipment. (Author's collection.)

Stone and brick formed a steady foundation for the North Family residence. State transportation officials hope to hold an exhibit of artifacts discovered in the dig and publish a summary of their findings. After their dig was completed, the site was bulldozed to straighten out a curve in the highway. (Author's collection.)

An old-fashioned pump and marble-topped basin dating from the 1890s are still intact in a Marble Hall bathroom. Marble-topped tables from the era are also still in use, and the marble floors are holding up well. (Author's collection.)

A historical marker, erected by Otterbein and the Ohio Historical Society in 1997, stands across the road from New Bethany. Today most of Bethany is used for residences. Housekeeping department offices are located in the basement, as well as the Shaker Cellar, a shop that is opened once a week. (Author's collection.)

BIBLIOGRAPHY

Bauer, Cheryl, and Rob Portman. *Wisdom's Paradise: The Forgotten Shakers of Union Village.* Wilmington, OH: Orange Frazer Press, 2004.

Boice, Martha, Dale Covington, and Richard Spence. *Maps of the Shaker West: A Journey of Discovery.* Dayton, OH: Knot Garden Press, 1997.

Burress, Marjorie Byrnside, ed. *Whitewater, Ohio, Village of Shakers, 1824–1916.* Self published, 1979.

Clark, Thomas, and F. Gerald Ham. *Pleasant Hill and Its Shakers.* Pleasant Hill, KY: Shakertown Press, 1968.

Hooper, James W. *The Shaker Communities of Kentucky: Pleasant Hill and South Union.* Charleston, SC: Arcadia Publishing, 2006.

Hunt, Melba L. *Summers at Watervliet.* Kettering, OH: Kettering-Moraine Museum and Historical Society, 1985.

McNemar, Richard. *The Kentucky Revival.* New York: Edward O. Jenkins, 1846.

Neal, Julia. *By Their Fruits: The Story of Shakerism in South Union, Kentucky.* Chapel Hill, NC: University of North Carolina Press, 1947.

Peckham, Arline B. *Faces of the Spirit: A History of Otterbein Home 1912–1987.* Lebanon, OH: Otterbein-Lebanon Retirement Community, 1987.

Piercy, Caroline B. *The Valley of God's Pleasure.* New York: Stratford House, 1951.

Phillips, Hazel Spencer. *Richard the Shaker.* Oxford, OH: Typoprint, 1972.

———. *Shaker Architecture.* Oxford, OH: Typoprint, 1971.

Townsley, Gardner H. *Historic Lebanon.* Lebanon, OH: Self published, 1965.

Van Houten, Ellen F., and Florence Cole. *Union Village Shakers, Warren County, Ohio, 1805–1920.* Loveland, OH: Cardinal Research, 2003.

ACROSS AMERICA, PEOPLE ARE DISCOVERING
SOMETHING WONDERFUL. *THEIR HERITAGE.*

Arcadia Publishing is the leading local history publisher in the United States. With more than 3,000 titles in print and hundreds of new titles released every year, Arcadia has extensive specialized experience chronicling the history of communities and celebrating America's hidden stories, bringing to life the people, places, and events from the past. To discover the history of other communities across the nation, please visit:

www.arcadiapublishing.com

Customized search tools allow you to find regional history books about the town where you grew up, the cities where your friends and family live, the town where your parents met, or even that retirement spot you've been dreaming about.